BISMILLAH,
LET'S EAT!

BISMILLAH, LET'S EAT!

Fresh and Vibrant Recipes from My Family to Yours

Go

hachette
BOOKS

New York

ZEHRA ALLIBHAI

PHOTOGRAPHY BY JOANNA WOJEWODA

Hachette Go, an imprint of Hachette Books
Hachette Book Group
1290 Avenue of the Americas
New York, NY 10104
HachetteGo.com
Facebook.com/HachetteGo
Instagram.com/HachetteGo

First Edition: October 2024

Published by Hachette Go, an imprint of Hachette Book Group, Inc. The Hachette Go name and logo is a trademark of the Hachette Book Group.

The Hachette Speakers Bureau provides a wide range of authors for speaking events. To find out more, go to hachettespeakersbureau.com or email HachetteSpeakers@hbgusa.com.

Hachette Go books may be purchased in bulk for business, educational, or promotional use. For information, please contact your local bookseller or Hachette Book Group Special Markets Department at special.markets@hbgusa.com.

The publisher is not responsible for websites (or their content) that are not owned by the publisher.

Library of Congress Cataloging-in-Publication Data

Names: Allibhai, Zehra, author. | Wojewoda, Joanna, photographer.
Title: Bismillah, let's eat!: fresh and vibrant recipes from my family to
    yours / by Zehra Allibhai; photography by Joanna Wojewoda.
Description: First edition. | New York, NY: Hachette Go, 2024. |
    Includes index.
Identifiers: LCCN 2023055664 | ISBN 9780306831119 (hardback) |
    ISBN 9780306831126 (ebook)
Subjects: LCSH: Cooking, Indic. | Cooking, Kenyan. | LCGFT: Cookbooks.
Classification: LCC TX724.5.I4 A745 2024 | DDC 641.5954—dc23/eng/
    20231207
LC record available at https://lccn.loc.gov/2023055664

ISBNs: 978-0-306-83111-9 (paper over board); 978-0-306-83112-6 (ebook)

Printed in China

IM

10 9 8 7 6 5 4 3 2 1

TO MY MOM (AKA: NANIMA TO MY KIDS),

who recognized that food was our love language

and proceeded to serve us endless portions of love.

Some of my most cherished memories while growing

up include eating your meals, which were a bridge

to our roots and heritage. I've always admired your

faith and dedication to our family and community.

Love you so much.

CONTENTS

LUNCH

SOUPS

SALADS

DINNER

SIDES & EXTRAS

DRINKS

SNACKS & TREATS

BISMILLAH,
LET'S EAT!

INTRODUCTION

BEFORE EATING, MUSLIMS PAUSE TO SAY "Bismillah." It means "I begin in the name of God." Similar to the practice of saying grace before a meal, it's a way to express gratitude for the food that we're about to eat and helps us set a mindful intention. I said it every day growing up with my parents, siblings, and grandmother, and now I say it every day with my own family. Food—and time spent around the table—has been at the center of all the best parts of my life.

This book is more than just a collection of recipes. It's a reflection of my love for food and how it has always brought me joy and comfort. Whether it's a recipe passed down through generations of my family or a dish inspired by our travels around the world, each one holds a special place in my heart.

I grew up spending hours in our Toronto kitchen with my mother and grandmother, learning the recipes that are particular to Indians in East Africa (my family's heritage). I learned how to make delicious dishes like Kuku Paka, biryani, and kachumber—as well as build deep family bonds. I marveled at the way my mother was able to not only make cooking look so effortless but also create meals that made our family feel so wonderfully cared for. Many of the recipes in this book come from my sweet mom, which, in turn, were passed down from her mother.

When I met my husband, Zee, one of our first connections was our shared love of food. Having grown up eating my family's traditional food, it was thrilling to expand our palates together. Given that we also both love to travel, eating our way through different countries quickly became one of our favorite forms of adventure.

Building our family was an adventure of a different kind! We now have two kids, Ahmed and Asiyah, and even before they joined us at the table I knew that I wanted them to be adventurous eaters. In South Asian families, "eating well" is very important. If I pick up my kids from my parents' place, my mom won't tell me if they were well behaved, she'll tell me how well they ate. It's a thing. Luckily, both my kids enjoy eating as much as I do and are open to trying new things, so they've developed far more sophisticated palates than I had at their age. And now I have the joy of passing on our family recipes to them. It's wonderful to see the joy and excitement in their faces as they connect with their heritage while adding their own twist to the recipes.

All the chapters of my life have influenced how I cook now. I love re-creating my family's traditional dishes, and I also love to make recipes that remind us of some of the memorable trips we've been on and what we ate in different countries. But, as much as I love culinary adventures, I'm a busy working mom, so I need a lot of recipes in my back pocket that come together easily. I also like recipes that can be used in different ways (like the butter chicken to pizza trick you'll find on page 73). And while the recipes must be memorable and easy, they must also be nourishing. I have a background in the health and fitness industry, and through my website, the FitNest, and my social media accounts, I've built a place for people to come for tools to live their healthiest lives possible. While this is definitely not a "diet" book, food is fuel for your journey, and my goal is to offer you dishes that make you feel good and give you energy for whatever your day brings. This is especially true during Ramadan (the month of fasting) when food plays such a pivotal role and cooking becomes as much a form of celebration as it is a means of sustenance. If you observe Ramadan, I've included a Ramadan Guide on pages 257–259 to help you prepare, with helpful meal suggestions for Suhoor, Iftaar, and Eid.

Some of you may find these dishes and ingredients very familiar. And some may find them new and perhaps even a bit intimidating. I hope you'll feel encouraged to try some new things—I think you'll surprise yourself at how easy it really is. Promise me you won't worry about perfection. Trust me. It's the least important part of cooking. Okay, maybe after you've been making roti for as many years as my mom, you'll perfect it. But remember what I said, the most important part of her food— and mine, and yours—is the love that's poured into it.

KITCHEN STAPLES

I ALWAYS KEEP MY PANTRY AND FRIDGE STOCKED with particular staples (beyond the usual suspects like oils, butter, and flour). Below I've listed my favorites, along with some helpful tips. You may already keep many of these items on hand. If anything isn't already on your shelves, add some to your own kitchen as your time, budget, and meal plan allow.

DRY HERBS AND SPICES

A well-stocked spice cabinet makes cooking so much more enjoyable. As herbs and spices lend the flavors that make these recipes so distinctive, it's worth taking a look at each of them in a bit more detail.

Achar pickle mix: See "Pickle mix."

Bay leaves: Incorporate bay leaves into dishes that are cooked slowly (like soups and sauces).

Black pepper, whole peppercorns or ground: I prefer to use a pepper mill while cooking. Freshly ground pepper is so much more flavorful and aromatic than preground pepper! But either will work in these recipes.

Cardamom, pods and ground: While you may be more familiar with the ground spice, cardamom always begins in the form of a pod. Cardamom pods can be used in recipes to infuse a dish with flavor while cooking and discarded before serving (much as you do with bay leaves). Before adding the cardamom pod to a dish, use the heel of your hand to crush the pod under the flat side of a knife—but not too hard, or the seeds will fall out! Just apply pressure until you hear a crunch.

Cinnamon, ground and stick: I keep both ground and stick cinnamon on hand. Ground cinnamon is essential for baking, as well as sprinkling on sweet dishes. Stick cinnamon infuses slow-cooked dishes with warm flavor.

Cloves, whole and ground: A little can go a long way with cloves! Like cinnamon, ground cloves are often used in baking; whole cloves infuse dishes with flavor.

Coriander, ground and whole: Ground coriander, which comes as a fine powder, has a warm and slightly citrusy flavor. Whole coriander seeds can be broken up in a mortar and pestle or a spice grinder to be added to pickles and chutneys. Coriander comes from the same plant as cilantro.

Cumin, whole seeds and ground: I use both whole cumin seeds and ground cumin in recipes. If you like, you can buy just the seeds

and grind them fresh to use in recipes calling for ground cumin.

Curry leaves: These aromatic leaves have a slightly citrusy flavor (and are completely unrelated to curry powder!).

Curry powder: These spice blends are a wonderful shortcut for complex curry flavors.

Fenugreek leaves (mehthi): Dried like bay leaves, fenugreek leaves are a staple in Indian, Ethiopian, Egyptian, Turkish, and Persian cooking, and have a slightly nutty, herby flavor.

Garam masala: While its name means "hot spices," garam masala isn't necessarily very spicy or hot. It's the name for a warming spice blend that's very common in Indian

and Pakistani cuisine. There are many regional variations, though it often consists of ground coriander, cumin, cloves, cardamom, cinnamon, and black pepper.

Kashmiri chile, ground: Another Indian staple, Kashmiri chile powder has only slightly more heat than paprika.

Mustard seeds: Yellow mustard seeds are often used in pickles and chutneys, giving them a little bite, whereas black mustard seeds are used to add a pepperiness to curries.

Paprika, ground: This mild spice is made from ground chiles and gives flavor and a touch of color to dishes.

Pickle mix: Achar pickle mix and ready pickle mix are spice blends that are used for making pickled vegetables and fruits (see the Spices, Pickles & Chutneys chapter). They are available in a box or jar in most Indian or Pakistani grocery stores.

Red chile, ground: Indian red chile powder is quite different from the Tex-Mex chili powder that you may be used to, and so I've listed it as "ground red chile" in these recipes to avoid any confusion. It is made from ground whole dried chiles.

Saffron: The vivid red strands of saffron give a beautiful golden hue and a slightly sweet, distinctive taste to recipes. It is an expensive ingredient but worth a splurge.

Salt: I use sea salt in my kitchen, but whatever you have on hand will be fine.

Sumac, ground: Sumac is an essential spice in Middle Eastern cooking. It has a slightly tangy, earthy flavor.

Turmeric, ground: This spice with a rusty orange hue gives an earthy and pleasantly bitter flavor to recipes.

Za'atar: This Middle Eastern spice blend has herbs (typically oregano and/or thyme) with sumac and sesame seeds.

PANTRY AND FRIDGE STAPLES

Beyond dried rice and beans, here are a few dry ingredients you'll need for these recipes.

Ambli: Ambli is a mixture of tamarind paste, sugar, spices, and water. This tangy condiment can be used in many ways, like a dip for samosas or drizzle for a wrap. You can make ambli, but it's so much easier to buy it at an Indian grocery store.

Cacao powder: Cacao powder is made from fermented, unroasted cacao beans (whereas cocoa powder, which you might be more familiar with, is made from beans that have been fermented, roasted, and processed at a higher temperature). As a result, cacao powder contains more nutrients than cocoa.

Chia seeds: Chia seeds are a great source of healthy fats, protein, and fiber. In liquid, these little seeds take on a gel-like consistency that is great in Chia Seed Pudding (page 30) and Overnight Oats (page 33). I store my seeds in the fridge in an airtight container.

Chickpea flour (gram flour or besan): This flour made of stone-ground chickpeas creates a crispy texture in recipes like fritters.

Coconut milk: This creamy and slightly sweet milk comes in tins and should be shaken before opening. I choose full-fat versions.

Eno: Eno is a fruit salt sold as an antacid. It comes in different flavors and is sometimes used like baking powder in Indian cooking. If you don't have Eno, baking soda will do!

Fried crispy onions: You can find fried crispy onions at most Indian grocery stores, or check online.

Semolina flour (soji): This slightly coarse grained flour gives a nutty flavor to rotis.

OILS AND FATS

In my recipes calling for neutral oil, you can choose vegetable oil, canola oil, or avocado oil.

Olive oil is another staple. Additionally, you may want to purchase the following:

Coconut oil: I like to use coconut oil in many recipes as a healthy and delicious alternative to butter.

Ghee: Ghee, or clarified butter, is a staple in Indian cooking. It can withstand higher temperatures than regular butter. You can buy it premade or DIY by melting butter in a saucepan, then bringing it to a gentle boil until foam rises to the top and then sinks to the bottom. Strain it and voilà! You have ghee.

KITCHEN TOOLS

MY RECIPES DON'T CALL FOR MANY SPECIAL tools beyond an Instant Pot, but here are some that can help you have success with these recipes.

Air fryer: This is a great tool for a healthier kitchen. Make crispy veggies and proteins without added oils.

Food processor: Food processors are your friends for chopping, puréeing, and mixing foods. With the right attachments, they can also make prepping veggies a breeze.

High-speed blender: A powerful blender can make quick work of even the toughest veggies.

Mandoline: A mandoline is great for thin, uniform slices of fruits and vegetables (I love to use one for making salads and slaws).

Mesh strainer: A fine-mesh strainer is useful for straining homemade nut and oat milk as well as soaked rice and lentils.

Multifunction pressure cooker or Instant Pot: If you add just one special tool to your kitchen, I think an Instant Pot should be it. They're so helpful for cooking proteins like meats, chicken, and dry beans in a fraction of the time it would take to slow cook.

Popsicle mold: You may want to freeze my Healthy-ish Mango Kulfi (page 246) as frozen pops, and to do that, you'll need a popsicle mold. (Honestly, I believe everybody, not just those who make food for children, should have one!)

Tawa: A tawa is a very shallow metal pan with many uses, but especially cooking Indian flatbreads like rotis, parathas, and chapatis. In Indian cultures, both the convex and concave sides of the pan are used for cooking. For the recipes in this book, you can absolutely cook those flatbreads in a regular skillet or frying pan. But I love to use my tawa.

YOU MAY RECOGNIZE MANY OF THESE RECIPES as condiments that you've seen in grocery stores or restaurants. And they are delicious as toppings or accompaniments for many dishes. But their true superpower is as flavor boosters in dishes. Adding any of them to your cooking will deliver an amazing depth of flavor, and you may just find yourself racing for them more and more!

GARLIC PASTE AND GINGER PASTE

I'm all about saving time and money in the kitchen. So many of the South Asian recipes in this book use some combination of garlic or ginger, and so having these pastes on hand is super convenient. They can be refrigerated (and even stored in the freezer), so you can always have them on hand to add flavor to your dishes. Making your own garlic paste is so easy and so much better than store-bought paste. If a recipe calls for grated garlic or ginger, you can swap in the same amount of paste.

GARLIC PASTE

MAKES ABOUT
3½ CUPS

1 pound garlic (12 to
  15 heads of garlic), peeled
2 tablespoons neutral
  oil, such as avocado or
  canola
2 teaspoons water

In a blender or food processor, place the garlic, oil, and water and blend to a smooth paste, scraping down the sides as needed.

Store in an airtight container in the fridge for up to 2 weeks or in the freezer for up to 6 months. If you're freezing it, portion the paste into tablespoon-sized dollops on a parchment-lined baking sheet, freeze, then transfer the frozen cubes into a plastic bag or container to freeze.

GINGER PASTE

MAKES ABOUT
3½ CUPS

1 pound ginger, peeled and
  chopped into chunks
2 tablespoons neutral
  oil, such as avocado or
  canola
2 teaspoons water

In a blender or food processor, place the ginger, oil, and water and blend to a smooth paste, scraping down the sides as needed.

Store in an airtight container in the fridge for up to 2 weeks or in the freezer for up to 6 months. If you're freezing it, portion the paste into tablespoon-sized dollops on a parchment-lined baking sheet, freeze, then transfer the frozen cubes into a plastic bag or container to freeze.

GREEN CHUTNEY

This spicy green chutney is a staple in my fridge. I didn't realize how often I used it until I started sharing my recipes online. I'd say, "Add in a teaspoon of green chutney," and people would ask, "What's that?" So, here it is. While it works well as a condiment for many dishes, like eggs, and in sandwiches and wraps, it also makes a tasty addition to so many other recipes. It's such a simple way to add that extra layer of flavor to your marinades and curries.

If you find it too spicy on its own, try mixing it in with some yogurt to make a perfect dip! A tablespoon of chutney to ½ cup plain yogurt is an excellent ratio.

MAKES ABOUT 1 CUP

---

2 bunches cilantro, hard stems removed, roughly chopped
4–6 green chiles (see Note)
1 tablespoon grated ginger
3 garlic cloves, peeled
2 teaspoons cumin seeds
1 teaspoon salt
1 tablespoon lemon juice
¼ cup water

In a blender, place all the ingredients and blend well, scraping down the sides as needed, until everything is well combined like a spicy smoothie!

Store in an airtight container in the fridge for 2 weeks or in the freezer for up to 6 months.

NOTE: I find the smaller the chiles, the spicier they are. Adjust the number you use based on how hot they are and your level of spice preference.

COCONUT CHUTNEY

This rich, cooling chutney goes perfectly with so many appetizers—it's a perfect condiment for samosas, dholka, bhajia, and channa! You can make a large batch, portion the chutney out into mason jars, and freeze the rest.

MAKES ABOUT 2 CUPS

1 bunch cilantro, hard
   stems removed, roughly
   chopped
4 green chiles
1 garlic clove, peeled
1 teaspoon salt
¼ cup water
2 cups unsweetened
   shredded coconut
Juice of 1 lime

In a blender or food processor, place the cilantro, chiles, garlic, salt, and water and blend into a paste, scraping down the sides as needed. Add the coconut and blend until everything is well combined. Add the lime juice and mix well.

Store the chutney in an airtight container in the fridge for up to 2 weeks or in the freezer for up to 3 months.

MASALA SPICE MIX

This harmonious blend of aromatic spices creates a deeply flavorful seasoning that can be used in many different ways.

MAKES ½ CUP

2 tablespoons ground coriander
2 tablespoons paprika
1 tablespoon ground cumin
1 teaspoon fenugreek leaves (mehthi)
1 teaspoon ground red chile
1 teaspoon ground Kashmiri chile
1 teaspoon ground ginger
1 teaspoon ground turmeric
½ teaspoon ground nutmeg
½ teaspoon ground cinnamon
¼ teaspoon ground cardamom
¼ teaspoon ground black pepper
1 teaspoon mace

In a medium bowl, place all the ingredients and mix well. Pour into an airtight jar.

The spice mix will keep in your pantry, out of direct sunlight, for up to 6 months.

TANDOORI MIX

This mix of spices will be a party for your senses! "Tandoori anything" is a hit in our house, and I'm guessing if you love spicy, aromatic foods, it will be one in yours as well. Making it at home means you can add just the right amount of kick that you like, plus you'll be avoiding all the unpleasant extras (food coloring, preservatives, and other chemicals) that none of us really need.

You can make a large batch of this spice blend and have it ready to use as a rub, or add it to yogurt and lemon for a delicious tandoori marinade. It's perfect to add to chicken, shrimp, fish, and tofu!

MAKES ⅓ TO ½ CUP

2 teaspoons ground coriander
2 teaspoons ground cumin
2 teaspoons garam masala
2 teaspoons ground ginger
2 teaspoons paprika
2 teaspoons ground turmeric
2 teaspoons garlic powder
1½ teaspoons ground black pepper
1 teaspoon ground cardamom
1 teaspoon salt
1 teaspoon ground red chile
1 teaspoon ground Kashmiri chile

Mix all the spices together and keep in an airtight container for up to 6 months.

GAJAR ATHANO
(Pickled Carrots)

Known as athano, pickled carrots are a delicious and easy way to add a flavorful and crunchy twist to any dish. The simple pickling process preserves the carrots' natural sweetness and crunch while infusing them with tangy, savory flavor. Although they're often paired with biryani, pilau, and other rice or curry dishes, I also love having them with my eggs at breakfast. The carrots will last for weeks (if not months) in an airtight container in the fridge, so you can make a big batch and enjoy it for many meals to come.

MAKES ABOUT 3 CUPS

3 large carrots, cut into matchsticks
1 green chile, sliced lengthwise very thin
2 tablespoons cilantro, finely chopped
1½ teaspoons ground red chile
1 teaspoon tomato paste
1 teaspoon salt
2 tablespoons lemon juice
2 tablespoons neutral oil

Place the chopped carrots in a large bowl. In a smaller bowl, combine the rest of the ingredients to make a loose paste. Pour the paste over the carrots and give everything a stir. Allow the carrots to sit for 10 minutes before serving.

Store in an airtight container for up to 3 weeks.

Keri Athano, p. 23   (TOP) Sambharo, p. 25   Gobi Athano, p. 22

(BOTTOM) Limbu Athano, p. 24

GOBI ATHANO
(Cauliflower Pickle)

This cauliflower pickle is something you'll always find in my fridge. I love its tangy, savory flavors! It's a great way to add a few more veggies onto your plate, and it takes simple fried eggs and toast to a whole other level.

MAKES ABOUT 8 CUPS

2 tablespoons salt
1 head cauliflower, cut into small florets
5 carrots, cut into sticks
3 tablespoons crushed yellow mustard seeds
2 tablespoons ground red chile
1½ teaspoons ground turmeric
¼ cup ready pickle mix
1–1¼ cups apple cider vinegar

In a colander, sprinkle 1 tablespoon of the salt over the cauliflower. In another colander, sprinkle the carrot sticks with the remaining salt. Let the veggies rest for 20 minutes to drain any excess water.

Meanwhile, in a large bowl, combine the mustard seeds, ground red chile, turmeric, pickle mix, and vinegar. Add the cauliflower and carrots and stir to coat the vegetables in the pickling spices.

Transfer the pickles to mason jars or clean jars. Store in the fridge for up to 2 months.

KERI ATHANO
(Green Mango Pickle)

I love the tartness of green mangoes. Pairing them with whole spices and chiles creates a winning combination that you might have never had before!

You will have extra pickle paste (made from the oil and spices), as you'll need only 5 tablespoons of it to make the keri athano. The paste can be used to make more batches of pickles, or you can even use it as a condiment, somewhat like a chile oil. Store it in a jar or airtight container in the fridge for up to 3 months.

MAKES ABOUT 4 CUPS

- 1 large unripe green mango, skin on, cut into 1-inch cubes
- 2 medium carrots, peeled and cut into 1-inch cubes
- 6–8 green chiles, halved lengthwise
- 2 cups canola oil
- 1 tablespoon minced fresh garlic
- 1 cup coarsely ground coriander seeds
- 2 teaspoons fenugreek seeds, coarsely ground
- 1 tablespoon crushed yellow mustard seeds
- 1 tablespoon salt
- 1½ tablespoons ground red chile
- ½ teaspoon ground turmeric
- 5 tablespoons achar pickle mix

Lay the mango, carrot, and chile pieces flat on a baking sheet. Place them in the sun or near a heater to dry for 12 to 16 hours.

Heat the oil in a small saucepan over medium-high heat. Once it begins to bubble, add the garlic and cook for about 30 seconds, then add the coriander seeds and stir well for 30 seconds.

Remove the pan from the heat. Let it cool for 3 minutes, and then add the fenugreek seeds and let the oil cool to room temperature, for about 20 minutes, to allow the flavor from the seeds to infuse the oil. Stir in the rest of the ingredients. Your mixture should have a paste-like consistency. Transfer the paste to a jar for storage.

Transfer the dried mango, carrots, and chiles to a large bowl. Add 5 tablespoons of the pickle paste and stir to coat. Transfer your pickles to jars and store them in the fridge for 1 month.

LIMBU ATHANO
(Lemon Pickle)

Bursting with flavor, this tart, spicy, and slightly sweet lemon pickle is a party in your mouth! I love adding this to curries for just a little extra kick of tartness and spice.

MAKES ABOUT 4 CUPS

5 tablespoons sugar
2 tablespoons achar pickle mix
2 tablespoons red pepper flakes
1½ tablespoons ground red chile
1 tablespoon salt
1 teaspoon ground turmeric
6 lemons, peels on, cut into 1-inch pieces
3–5 small green chiles, halved lengthwise
1 (2-inch) piece fresh ginger, peeled and cut into small pieces

In a large microwave-safe bowl, combine the sugar, pickle mix, red pepper flakes, ground red chile, salt, and turmeric. Microwave on high for 3 minutes, stir, and microwave for another 3 minutes until the mixture thickens enough to cling to the back of a spoon.

Stir again and let the mixture cool for 10 minutes. Add the lemon pieces, green chiles, and ginger and stir to coat well. Once the pickles have cooled completely, spoon into jars and keep in the fridge for up to 2 months.

SAMBHARO
(Carrot and Green Mango Pickle)

I could eat these carrot pickles by the jar. The carrots are cooked slightly to soften them while still keeping them crunchy. Cooking the spices with a little tomato paste makes sambharo a little milder than the other pickles in this book. Pair it with rice, dal, paratha—anything that needs a little pick-me-up.

MAKES ABOUT 4 CUPS

½ cup neutral oil

2 teaspoons black mustard seeds

3 large carrots, peeled and cut into strips 1½ × ¼ inches

1 large green mango, skin on, cut into strips 1½ × ¼ inches

10 green chiles, sliced in half lengthwise

2 tablespoons achar pickle mix

2 tablespoons crushed tomato

1 teaspoon tomato paste

1 teaspoon garlic paste (page 13)

1 teaspoon salt

1 teaspoon ground red chile

¼ teaspoon ground turmeric

Heat the oil in a large pot over medium heat. When it starts to bubble, add the mustard seeds and cook until they pop. Stir in the carrots until well coated. Cover the pot and cook for 5 minutes until the carrots are slightly softened. Turn off the heat and add the mango, chiles, and the remaining ingredients. Stir well.

Allow the mixture to cool completely before transferring it into jars. The pickles will keep in the fridge for 3 to 4 weeks.

BREAKFAST

I HAVE A CONFESSION TO MAKE: MY NAME IS Zehra and I am a morning person. I love getting up while the house is still quiet to get my workout in, have a coffee, and get my thoughts together for the day. Doesn't that sound peaceful and lovely? It is . . . until my family gets up. On weekdays, there's always a brief period of chaos as everyone has breakfast, lunches get packed, homework needs to be found, and we're all out the door. But on the weekends, we like to make breakfast or brunch a feast to be lingered over with our friends and extended family. Whether you need something lightning fast for the most hectic mornings or a hearty dish to serve to a gang, I've got you covered.

CHOCOLATE DATE GRANOLA

Making your own granola means you get to put in *exactly* what you want (and you can avoid all the extra sugar and stuff you don't). Once you've got a recipe down, it's super easy to customize, but do give this combo a try at least once—coconut, oats, nuts, dates, and chocolate are such a dreamy mix. And, as an added bonus, your kitchen will smell amazing when that pan hits the oven. This granola is delicious on its own, with milk, or in the Granola Yogurt Parfait (page 245).

MAKES 6 CUPS

3 cups rolled oats
1 cup shredded coconut
1 cup whole almonds
1 cup pumpkin seeds
⅓ cup hemp hearts
⅓ cup pecans or walnuts
1 teaspoon ground
  cinnamon
½ teaspoon salt
¾ cup maple syrup
⅓ cup melted coconut oil
1 teaspoon vanilla extract
5–6 medjool dates, pitted
  and chopped
¼ cup dark chocolate
  chips or chopped dark
  chocolate

Preheat the oven to 325°F. Line two rimmed baking sheets with parchment paper.

In a bowl, combine the oats, coconut, almonds, pumpkin seeds, hemp hearts, pecans, cinnamon, and salt and stir to mix.

In a large liquid measuring cup, combine the syrup, coconut oil, and vanilla. Drizzle the wet ingredients over the dry mixture and stir to coat.

Spread out the granola on the prepared baking sheets. Bake for 25 minutes, stirring after every 8 to 10 minutes, until everything is nice and toasted. Keep an eye on it because it can burn quickly.

Let the granola cool completely on the pan. Stir in the dates and chocolate. The granola will keep in an airtight container for up to 10 days.

CHIA SEED PUDDING

Chia seeds are a great source of healthy fats, protein, and fiber, which will help keep you feeling full and satisfied throughout the morning. One tip for making this dish even better is to use almond milk instead of regular milk to add a rich and creamy flavor to the dish. Also, you can use different types of sweeteners like maple syrup or coconut sugar to give it a different flavor.

Here's the recipe for one serving, though you can multiply it for the ultimate meal-prep breakfast. I make a big batch on the weekend, and on busy mornings everyone will just grab a jar as they head out the door. Sometimes I'll make half of them plain and the other half chocolate—or even layer the chocolate and plain pudding in one jar so it's a treat for the eyes as well as the taste buds!

MAKES 1 SERVING

CHIA PUDDING

1¼ cups almond milk, coconut milk, or any other milk of your choice
3 tablespoons chia seeds
1 teaspoon maple syrup
½ teaspoon vanilla extract
½ teaspoon ground cinnamon
1 tablespoon cacao powder or nut butter (optional)

TOPPING SUGGESTIONS

Fresh or dried fruit
Seeds
Nuts
Shredded coconut

Place all the ingredients except your toppings in a glass jar and mix well with a spoon—make sure you incorporate all the chia seeds that settle at the bottom. Or close the jar and give it a little shake. Place it in the fridge overnight (or for at least 3 hours). The chia seeds will thicken up and create a pudding-like consistency. Enjoy as is or with toppings if you like.

TIP: Here are some of my fave topping combos—

Strawberry, banana, and mango

Banana and peanut butter

Coconut, pomegranate seeds, and blueberries

OVERNIGHT OATS (FIVE WAYS)

This is another great breakfast you can easily prep ahead of time. Simply letting them sit overnight allows the oats to soak up and soften in the liquid so you don't have to cook them. All you'll have to do in the morning is give them a good stir and add your toppings. It's that easy!

You can enjoy them plain or topped with fruits and nuts. Try some of the great variations below, or make up your own delicious combo!

BASIC OVERNIGHT OATS

MAKES 3 SERVINGS

1 cup Greek yogurt or skyr
1 cup rolled oats
1½ cups almond milk, coconut milk, or any other milk of your choice
¼ cup chia seeds
1 tablespoon maple syrup or honey
½ teaspoon vanilla extract

In a large bowl, combine all the ingredients and mix well. Stir in the optional flavor additions if desired. If you wish, divide the oats between smaller airtight containers. Cover and refrigerate at least 4 hours or overnight until the oats have softened.

The oats will keep in the fridge for a week.

TIPS: If you're making the Tropical Dream Overnight Oats, reserve the fresh mango to top the oats just before serving; if you like your oats less sweet, you can adjust or eliminate the maple syrup.

OPTIONAL FLAVOR VARIATIONS

TROPICAL DREAM OVERNIGHT OATS

2 tablespoons fresh orange juice
¼ cup grated green apple
2 tablespoons coconut flakes
1 tablespoon passion fruit pulp
Fresh mango for topping

COFFEE OVERNIGHT OATS

½ teaspoon brown sugar
¼ cup regular espresso or cold-brew coffee
Pinch of sea salt

CARROT CAKE OVERNIGHT OATS

¼ cup shredded carrot
1 tablespoon shredded coconut
1 tablespoon raisins
½ teaspoon ground cinnamon

PB & J OVERNIGHT OATS

1 tablespoon raspberry jam or purée
1 tablespoon peanut butter or almond butter
1 teaspoon chopped peanuts

SAFFRON OATMEAL

This creamy flavorful oatmeal tastes like a hug in a bowl. Adding just a few spices can make a world of difference compared to your regular oats. I'm pretty sure my mom invented this breakfast and the whole family fell in love. When we're all visiting, she makes the oatmeal the night before and we sit at the table in the morning and enjoy our oats.

MAKES 2 TO 3 SERVINGS

OATMEAL

1 cup rolled oats
1 cup water
1 cup milk of choice
2 teaspoons ground cinnamon
1 cardamom pod
¼ cup maple syrup
Pinch of saffron

TOPPING SUGGESTIONS

Fresh or dried fruit
Nuts
Seeds
Nut butter
Chopped dark chocolate

Combine the oats and water in a medium saucepan. Bring them to a simmer over medium heat for 1 to 2 minutes. Add the milk and cook for 5 to 7 minutes or until the oats are quite soft. Add the cinnamon, cardamom pod, maple syrup, and saffron. Stir and cook for another minute or two. Remove the cardamom pod before serving. Divide the oatmeal between serving bowls and add any toppings if desired.

CHOCOLATE CHIP BANANA BLENDER PANCAKES

I've been making these pancakes since the kids were young and they're still a hit! I love that you can just toss everything into the blender and have a yummy stack of light and healthy pancakes ready to go in no time. Got some bananas browning on your kitchen counter? Toss 'em in the blender and they'll give the pancakes a natural sweetness that's hard to resist. Also, you can use dark and milk chocolate chips to give a variety of flavors. Serve them with berries and maple syrup on top. One taste and you'll say goodbye to boxed pancake mix too!

MAKES 12 TO 16 PANCAKES

2 ripe bananas
3 eggs
2 cups rolled oats
⅓ cup milk
1½ tablespoons maple syrup
1½ teaspoons ground cinnamon
1½ teaspoons vanilla extract
1½ teaspoons baking powder
⅓ cup chocolate chips
1 teaspoon coconut oil

In a blender, place everything except the chocolate chips and coconut oil and blend until well combined. Stir in the chocolate chips.

Melt the coconut oil in a frying pan over medium-high heat, and pour in some of the batter, about ¼ cup per pancake. Depending on the size of your pan, you can cook two to three pancakes at a time. Let the pancakes cook until bubbles start to form along the edges, then flip them over and cook for another minute until cooked through. Repeat with the remaining batter until all the pancakes are cooked.

TIP: Leftover pancakes will keep in an airtight container in the fridge for up to 5 days. They also freeze really well. Just take them out the night before, thaw in the fridge, and pop them in the toaster to heat up when you're ready to eat!

MASALA OMELET

This is Zee's favorite weekend meal: a quick and easy omelet bursting with Indian flavor. It's great with paratha or white bread, folded into a bun (in the style of Indian street food!), on its own, or along with some chutney for a great breakfast on the go. Using ghee adds rich flavor and healthy fats, but butter works just as well.

MAKES 4 SERVINGS

5 eggs
1 tablespoon milk
1 teaspoon ground red chile
½ teaspoon salt
½ teaspoon ground black
   pepper
1½ teaspoons butter or ghee
1 small onion, chopped
1 medium tomato, chopped
1 small green chile, chopped
1 tablespoon chopped
   cilantro

Crack the eggs into a large bowl. Whisk in the milk, ground red chile, salt, and pepper.

Melt the butter or ghee in a medium frying pan over medium heat. Add the onion and cook till it begins to soften, 6 to 8 minutes, then stir in the tomato and green chile. Immediately add the egg mixture and lower the heat to medium-low. Let it cook until the edges start to firm up, then, with a spatula, gently pull the eggs away from the sides of the pan and allow the liquid in the center to run toward the edges. Cook for 4 to 5 minutes until almost cooked through. Sprinkle with cilantro and continue to cook until the eggs are cooked through.

Remove the pan from the heat. Cut the omelet into quarters and serve.

EGG CUPS ON THE GO

This is my take on a certain popular coffee chain's egg bites. In case you couldn't tell, I'm a huge fan of breakfast dishes you can make ahead of time so that you can just grab and enjoy on the run! Feel free to mix up what veggies you add (pro tip: toss in any ingredients that are sitting in your fridge that need to be used up!). Aside from breakfast, these bites are an excellent post-workout snack when our bodies need a balance of protein and carbohydrates.

MAKES 12 EGG CUPS

2 cups chopped spinach
¼ cup chopped mushrooms
¼ cup quartered cherry
   tomatoes
8 eggs
¼ cup milk of choice
Salt and pepper to taste
½ cup shredded Cheddar or
   mozzarella cheese

Preheat the oven to 350°F. Thoroughly grease a twelve-cup muffin tin.

Divide your veggies evenly between the muffin cups.

In a large bowl, whisk the eggs, milk, and salt and pepper to taste. Transfer the egg mixture to a large, spouted measuring cup, which makes it easier to pour. Carefully pour the egg mixture over the veggies, filling each muffin cup three-quarters full—these babies rise! Top each egg cup with a little cheese.

Bake for 18 minutes until they are set. Let the muffins cool for about 5 minutes before removing them from the tin.

These muffins will last for a few days in an airtight container in the fridge. Reheat in the microwave or toaster oven.

TIP: Asiyah started drizzling her egg cups with Sriracha sauce; she was definitely on to something because now the rest of us do the same!

SPICY SHAKSHUKA

I'd say that shakshuka is the perfect breakfast food, but who am I kidding? I've pulled out this recipe for lunch and dinner also! Healthy and easy to make, this delicious dish of eggs poached in a flavorful tomato and pepper sauce is sure to be a crowd-pleaser and a new favorite in your recipe collection. It's typically served with crusty bread, which is a perfect way to sop up the delicious sauce. This is a dish you can really have fun with. Once you've got the basic recipe down, feel free to change it up by adding different veggies to the base or topping with different cheeses (feta works great too!). We usually like to kick up the spice level, but you can adjust to whatever heat your taste buds desire.

**MAKES 4 TO 6
SERVINGS**

2 tablespoons olive oil
1 yellow onion, chopped
2 garlic cloves, crushed
½ red bell pepper, chopped
2 teaspoons ground cumin
2 teaspoons smoked paprika
1 teaspoon red pepper
   flakes
1 teaspoon sumac
½ teaspoon salt
½ cup halved cherry
   tomatoes
1 (28-ounce) can crushed
   tomatoes
6 large eggs, at room
   temperature
¼ cup crumbled goat
   cheese or feta cheese
   (optional)
2–3 tablespoons chopped
   cilantro or parsley

Heat the oil in a large skillet over medium heat. Add the onion and garlic and sauté until fragrant, about 5 minutes. Add the bell pepper and cook until very soft, for 3 to 5 minutes.

Add the spices and salt and let them toast a little, about 1 minute. Stir in the cherry tomatoes and cook until they've broken down a bit, about 6 minutes, then add the crushed tomatoes and mix well. Lower the heat and let the tomato mixture simmer for 10 to 12 minutes until it thickens into a chunky sauce. Add water if it gets too dry. Taste the sauce and adjust for seasoning.

Set the heat to low and make six indents in the sauce with the back of a spoon. Crack an egg into each indent. The eggs may run a little, and that's okay! Let the eggs cook in the mixture until they begin to set, about 5 minutes. Cover the skillet with a lid and cook for 5 more minutes, or until the eggs reach your preferred doneness. Sprinkle the cheese on top, then cover again with the lid and cook for another minute until the cheese is slightly melted.

Remove from the heat and sprinkle with cilantro. Use a large spoon to carefully lift each portion so that the poached eggs stay intact.

EGGS WITH SWEET POTATO HASH

This recipe came about because I was craving sweet potato fries with my eggs but didn't want to worry about all the mess and waiting with deep-frying. So instead I tried shredding the sweet potatoes and cooking them up quickly, then adding the eggs right into the same pan. This dish is a perfect example of how simple ingredients can come together to create something truly delicious and satisfying. It brings out the natural sweetness of the sweet potatoes, and the caramelization gives them a crunchy exterior, which is rounded out with kale, paprika, and red pepper flakes for a touch of heat. This is one of my go-to breakfasts when I want something quick but filling. It's a great balanced meal full of protein and complex carbs that will give you energy throughout the day and have you feeling full longer!

MAKES 2 SERVINGS

1½ tablespoons coconut oil
1 small sweet potato, peeled and shredded
½ cup baby spinach leaves
1½ teaspoons paprika
1 teaspoon red pepper flakes, plus more for garnish
1 teaspoon salt
1 teaspoon ground black pepper
2 eggs
Chopped cilantro, for garnish

Melt the coconut oil in a large frying pan over medium-high heat. Add the sweet potato and cook, stirring constantly, until it starts to soften, about 5 minutes. Add your greens and spices and stir to combine. Continue cooking until the potato is cooked through and the spinach is softened, for 3 to 5 minutes. Spread the mixture into an even layer in the pan and make two little dents for the eggs with the back of a spoon.

Crack an egg into each hole and cook until the egg begins to set, about 5 minutes. Cover the pan and let the eggs cook to your preferred doneness. Carefully divide the mixture between two plates and garnish with some more crushed red pepper and cilantro.

TIP: You can shred the sweet potato the night before and keep it in an airtight container in the fridge.

POTATO CURRY WITH EGGS

This simple curry was one of the first of my mom's recipes that I learned to make when I was young, which makes it especially nostalgic for me. Whenever it was my turn to cook, I'd usually make this dish as it's pretty much foolproof—even more so now using an Instant Pot. The curry base is rich, tangy, and aromatic while the potatoes and eggs mean that it's hearty and satisfying. Now I can't wait for Ahmed and Asiyah to learn how to make this one!

MAKES 4 TO 5 SERVINGS

10 eggs
1–2 tablespoons neutral oil
2½ cups crushed or strained tomatoes
1 teaspoon salt
2½ teaspoons ground red chile
1½ teaspoons ground turmeric
5–6 medium potatoes, peeled and cut into 1½-inch cubes
Toasted bread, to serve

Bring a large pot of water to a boil. Gently lower in the eggs and boil for 10 minutes. Immediately transfer the eggs to an ice bath to cool them down.

While the eggs cool, make your potato curry. Select the SAUTÉ mode on your Instant Pot or pressure cooker and pour in the oil. Add the crushed tomatoes and spices and bring to a simmer. Allow the sauce to simmer until you see the oil beginning to separate on the edges, for 1 to 2 minutes. Add the chopped potatoes and stir to coat with the tomato sauce. Press CANCEL. Add ⅓ cup water, lock the lid into place, and set to sealing. Cook on high pressure for 5 minutes until the potatoes are fully cooked through. Release the pressure manually, press CANCEL, and remove the lid. If the curry looks too thick, just add a little more water.

While the curry is cooking, peel the hard-boiled eggs and slice them in half lengthwise. Divide the potato curry between serving bowls, top with the eggs, and enjoy with toasted bread.

NANIMA'S POTATO OMELET

Growing up, I awoke to the smell of this omelet cooking on most weekends, and my mom (whom our kids call "Nanima") still makes it for the kids whenever they stay over. First, the potatoes are diced and sautéed until they're perfectly tender, and then you add the spiced egg mixture. My mom would also pack it with onions, and we'd enjoy it with fresh paratha (a flatbread), yogurt, and green chutney; you can also serve it with Pickled Carrots (page 20). It's kinda like a frittata but with all the Indian spices to warm your soul (and your taste buds). I love that the kids gobble it up and that they're just as excited when they smell it cooking on a weekend morning as I was!

MAKES 4 SERVINGS

1½ tablespoons ghee or olive oil
2 medium potatoes, peeled and cut into 1-inch cubes
1 medium onion, thinly sliced
7 eggs
¼ cup milk
1 teaspoon salt
1 teaspoon ground black pepper
1 teaspoon ground red chile
1 small green chile, chopped (optional)
Chopped cilantro, for garnish

In a large skillet, heat 1 tablespoon of the ghee over medium heat. Add the potatoes and cook, stirring occasionally, until they are cooked halfway through, for 5 to 7 minutes. Add the onion and continue to cook, stirring occasionally, until the potatoes are cooked through and begin to brown, another 3 to 5 minutes.

While the potatoes are cooking, crack the eggs into a large bowl. Whisk in the milk, salt, pepper, and ground red chile until well combined.

Add the remaining ½ tablespoon ghee to the pan and mix so it's coating the bottom of the pan. Pour the egg mixture over the vegetables. Let it cook until the sides start to firm up, then, with a spatula, gently pull the eggs from the sides and tilt the pan to allow the liquid egg mixture from the center to run toward the edges of the pan. Cook until the eggs are set on the bottom, then cover with a lid and cook until the eggs are cooked through, for 4 to 6 minutes.

Remove the pan from the heat and cut the omelet into quarters. Sprinkle with the green chile, if desired, and the cilantro.

CHANA PARATHA WRAPS

I love having breakfast for dinner . . . but I also love having dinner for breakfast! I often repurpose leftovers from last night's dinner into a completely different dish. I like to add an egg for a little extra protein (totally optional), some greens to up the nutrition factor, and some chutney to round it all out. If you are not familiar with paratha, it is a flaky flatbread that can be served alongside dishes or as a wrap. This wrap will keep you going far longer than a bowl of cereal or a bagel.

Like a lot of my recipes, you can use the idea as your starting point and go from there. All you need is some paratha and last night's curry.

MAKES 2 SERVINGS

1 teaspoon neutral oil or ghee (optional)
2 eggs, beaten (optional)
½ cup Chana Bateta (Chickpea and Potato Curry) (page 80)
2 teaspoons green chutney (page 14)
2 tablespoons plain yogurt
2 paratha
2 tablespoons shredded mozzarella cheese
½ cup baby spinach
1–2 slices red onion (optional)
1–2 slices tomato (optional)
Chopped cilantro (optional)

If you'd like your wrap with an egg, heat the oil in a frying pan over medium heat. Pour in the egg and let it cook for 20 to 30 seconds without stirring so it begins to set. Stir the egg as it cooks until it is softly set in large curds of scrambled egg. Remove from the pan and set aside.

If your curry is cold, reheat it.

In a small bowl, mix the chutney and the yogurt to make a sauce.

Cut a slit in your paratha, just to the center of the circle. Place it in the frying pan over medium heat, with the cut coming down, as if at six o'clock. Imagine your paratha having four equal pie pieces. Spoon the curry onto one of the other pie pieces (don't worry about spillage!). Spoon the sauce on another pie piece, and arrange the spinach, onion, tomato, and cilantro to taste, if desired, on another. Sprinkle the first pie piece with the cheese and the egg, if using, and cook until the cheese melts slightly. With the cut facing you in the pan, fold the bottom two pie pieces up over the top two. Now fold those two triangles together so you have one four-layer triangle.

Remove the wrap from the pan, drizzle with the chutney sauce, and enjoy.

MASALA ROTI

These savory roti flatbreads have the spices cooked right in and are so packed with flavor that you can eat them on their own, or enjoy them with a meal any time of day. Try them with some eggs, yogurt, and green chutney, and you have a breakfast that makes it feel like you're eating out of a street food cart in Gujarat, India!

MAKES 12 ROTIS

2 cups whole wheat flour, plus more for dusting
½ cup fenugreek leaves (mehthi)
½ cup chopped cilantro
2 teaspoons salt
1 teaspoon ground coriander
1 teaspoon ground cumin
½ teaspoon ground turmeric
1 teaspoon ground red chile
1 teaspoon green chutney (page 14)
1 teaspoon garlic, minced
1 cup warm water
6 tablespoons canola oil
1 tablespoon ghee

In a large mixing bowl, combine all the ingredients except the ghee. Stir together to form a dough. Knead directly in the bowl until the dough becomes smooth. Cover the bowl with a tea towel, and let the dough rest for 10 to 15 minutes.

Dust your work surface with flour. Separate the dough into ten to twelve equal-sized balls.

Heat a large frying pan or tawa over medium-high heat.

Working one at a time, roll a ball of dough between your hands and flatten it into a circle. Dust on both sides with flour. With a rolling pin, roll the dough to a thin circle 5 to 6 inches in diameter, turning occasionally and applying a little pressure to flatten it. If the roti is sticking to the rolling pin or your work surface, dust with a little more flour.

Put the rolled-out dough into the hot pan. Cook for 30 seconds, then flip right away with a wooden spatula or your fingers (the first flip is always quick!). Cook a little longer on the second side, until the roti has brown spots, then flip once again. When you press down on the roti with a flat spatula, it will puff up.

Transfer the cooked roti from the pan to a plate and brush it with a little ghee. Cover it with a clean dish towel to keep it warm. Repeat the rolling, cooking, and brushing process with the remaining dough balls until all the rotis are cooked. The rotis are best eaten right away.

GRILLED CHEESE AVOCADO SANDWICH

Who says you can't have grilled cheese for breakfast? It's easy to make, nutritious, filling, and delicious, so it ticks all the boxes as far as I'm concerned! I love using sourdough bread because it adds depth with a tangy and slightly nutty flavor that pairs perfectly with the creamy avocado and melty cheese. Bonus tip if you're looking for that perfect cheese pull: try using mozzarella or havarti either on their own or mixed in with Cheddar cheese. Serve it with fresh fruit on the side for a great, well-rounded breakfast.

MAKES 1 SERVING

1 teaspoon butter, softened
2 large slices sourdough bread
3 slices Cheddar or mozzarella cheese
3–4 tomato slices
⅓ ripe avocado, sliced
Squeeze of lemon juice
1 teaspoon red pepper flakes
½ cup arugula or spinach leaves

Heat a frying pan over medium heat. Butter your bread slices on one side, then place one piece of bread, butter side down, in the hot pan. Layer on your cheese and cook until the bread is toasted and the cheese is melted, for 3 to 4 minutes. You can cover the pan with a lid if your cheese isn't melting quickly enough. Top the bread with the tomatoes, avocado, lemon juice, red pepper flakes, and arugula. Add the other slice of buttered bread on top, buttered side out, and flip the whole sandwich to toast the other side.

Slide your sandwich onto a plate. Cut it in half and enjoy!

TIP: For a lighter meal, use just one slice of bread and serve this as an open-faced sandwich.

LUNCH

LUNCH CAN LOOK VERY DIFFERENT DEPENDING

on the day and who's coming to the table. There are school and workdays, when you might be throwing meals into lunch boxes amid the hectic clatter of your morning routine. You want something that's quick and easy, but that will also be a rewarding break in the day and some good fuel for the rest of it. (My secret for those days is to use up leftovers from last night's dinner!) And then there are times when you can slow down and take your time in the kitchen and around the table. These recipes are my go-tos for both scenarios that will keep everyone, kids and grown-ups, satisfied until dinner.

GRILLED CHEESE STUFFED NAAN

If you like grilled cheese, this stuffed naan will blow your mind. It's got a spicy kick from the green chutney, and it will quickly become your go-to vegetarian sandwich. The quick raita on the side (made from green chutney and yogurt) takes it over the top! You can make the stuffed naan with your favorite cheese (I like mozzarella, Cheddar, or havarti) and, for a full meal experience, serve it with soup, such as my Creamy Coconut Lentil Soup (page 86) or Roasted Tomato Soup (page 92). If I'm having friends over for lunch, this combo is an instant hit.

MAKES 1 LARGE
STUFFED NAAN
(2 SERVINGS)

2 naan bread
Oil, ghee, or butter
1 tablespoon plus 1 teaspoon
   green chutney (page 14)
6 slices of your favorite
   cheese
1 medium tomato, cut into
   slices
½ cup baby spinach
¼ cup yogurt

Heat a large pan over medium heat. Spread both sides of the naan with oil and place in the pan to heat. Spread 1 tablespoon of the chutney onto the naan and top with three slices of cheese, then the tomatoes and spinach. Add the other three slices of cheese over the spinach and cover with the other piece of naan. Cook on low heat until the cheese begins to melt and the naan gets crispy, for 3 to 5 minutes, then flip the "naan sandwich" so the other side can brown and the cheese continues to melt, for 3 minutes more. Press the sandwich down with a flat spatula to make sure everything melts together.

While the sandwich cooks, mix the yogurt with the remaining 1 teaspoon chutney to make a raita dipping sauce.

Remove from the pan and allow the sandwich to cool a bit, then cut in half. Serve with the dipping sauce.

CHICKEN TIKKA WRAPS

A tikka marinade gives you chicken that is rich and flavorful with a delicate spice. You can do so much with this chicken. Grill it and have it handy for salads, add it to chicken masala curry, or put it into wraps for a delicious lunch, as I've done here.

Having marinated chicken tikka in your freezer is a game changer. I always buy chicken breasts in bulk at my butcher and ask him to cut them into small cubes. I marinate it all with this flavorful tikka marinade, section it into 2-pound portions, and freeze them in resealable bags. Then I can just take a bag out of the freezer in the morning and place it in cold water to thaw. By the time I'm ready to cook lunch, the chicken is thawed and I can whip up a delicious meal in no time.

MAKES 6 WRAPS

CHICKEN TIKKA

½ cup plain whole milk Greek or regular yogurt
2 garlic cloves, minced
1 tablespoon minced ginger
Juice of ½ lemon
1 teaspoon ground coriander
½ teaspoon ground turmeric
½ teaspoon ground cumin
1 teaspoon paprika
½ teaspoon ground red chile
1 teaspoon ground Kashmiri chile
Pinch of ground cinnamon
1 teaspoon salt
½ teaspoon ground black pepper
1 tablespoon canola oil
2 tablespoons chopped cilantro
3 boneless chicken breasts (about 2 pounds), chopped into 1½-inch cubes

In a large bowl, combine all the ingredients for the chicken tikka except for the chicken and stir until well combined. Add the chicken chunks and stir so that every piece is coated. Cover the bowl and place in the fridge for at least 2 hours—the longer it sits, the more flavorful it will be. After this step, you could put the marinated chicken into a resealable plastic freezer bag and freeze for up to 4 months.

Once you're ready to cook, thread four to five chicken cubes onto each wooden skewer until you've used up all your chicken. Brush your grill or pan with oil and bring it to medium-high heat. Cook the skewers until the chicken is cooked through and there are some nice char marks on the outside, for 3 to 4 minutes per side. Allow the chicken to cool slightly so you can remove it from the skewers.

In a small bowl, mix the yogurt and green chutney to make a creamy raita.

WRAPS

½ cup plain yogurt

1 tablespoon green chutney
  (page 14)

6 large naan (store-bought
  or see page 195) or
  paratha (page 48)

1 small onion, thinly sliced

1 medium tomato, chopped

1 cup shredded iceberg
  lettuce

2 tablespoons ambli

To make a wrap, spread some of the raita on a naan, place one chicken skewer (stick removed!) on top, and top with onions, tomatoes, and lettuce. Add a drizzle of ambli. Repeat with the remaining wrap ingredients.

MEAN GREEN TUNA SALAD SANDWICH

I make this easy tuna salad for the kids at least once a week: it's simple but super tasty and a great way to get in a bunch of healthy greens. Between the avocado, the spinach, the cucumber, and the cilantro, it does have a decidedly green hue—so I tell them it's a Hulk Sandwich! Serve it on sandwich rolls with a side of chips.

MAKES 4 REGULAR
SANDWICHES OR
2 LARGE ROLLS

TUNA SALAD

1 (5-ounce) can water-
   packed tuna, drained
½ avocado
1 tablespoon mayonnaise
1 teaspoon grainy mustard
1 cup chopped fresh spinach
1–2 small cucumbers,
   chopped
¼ cup chopped cilantro
1 teaspoon salt
1 teaspoon ground black
   pepper
1 tablespoon ground cumin
Juice of ½ lemon
1 teaspoon lemon zest

SANDWICHES

2 sandwich rolls
Lettuce leaves or baby
   spinach (optional)
Sliced tomato (optional)
Sliced cucumber (optional)

In a large bowl, mix all the tuna salad ingredients until well combined. The texture is totally up to you: you can keep it a little chunky or mix it into an almost whipped consistency. Scoop tuna onto sandwich rolls and top with greens and any other toppings you like!

SALMON TERIYAKI BOWLS

These bowls are almost too pretty to eat, but one taste of the sweet and savory marinade and you won't hesitate to dig right in. For a fun weekend lunch, put out the toppings as a DIY salmon bowl bar, and everyone can fix their bowls just the way they like.

SERVES 2 GENEROUSLY

SALMON AND MARINADE

2 skinless salmon fillets
2 tablespoons soy sauce
1 tablespoon rice vinegar
1 tablespoon oyster sauce
1 tablespoon maple syrup
1 tablespoon grated ginger
1 tablespoon minced garlic
1 teaspoon red pepper flakes
1 teaspoon sesame seeds
2 tablespoons neutral oil

TOPPINGS

Jasmine rice (½ cup per bowl)
Sliced avocado
Edamame
Shredded carrot
Sliced green onion
Sesame seeds or furikake
Japanese mayo

Slice the salmon fillets into 1½-inch cubes.

In a large bowl or pie plate, combine the soy sauce, vinegar, oyster sauce, maple syrup, ginger, garlic, red pepper flakes, and sesame seeds. Add the salmon and turn to coat. Marinate for 10 minutes at room temperature. Remove the salmon and retain the marinade.

Heat the oil in a frying pan over medium heat. Cook the salmon for 1 to 2 minutes per side to sear. Add the marinade and cook until the salmon is nice and flaky. Since these are cubes, they will cook quickly.

To assemble the bowls, spoon some rice into the bottom of each bowl. Top with some of the salmon and your desired toppings. Or serve the toppings buffet style.

LOADED SWEET POTATOES

If you're looking for a satisfying lunch that's packed with protein and filling complex carbs, these loaded sweet potatoes are for you! This recipe is a delicious way to switch up leftovers from my tuna salad (page 61), Butter Chicken (page 158), or Tex-Mex Shredded Chicken Tacos (page 74). This recipe calls for two sweet potatoes, but you could make more, keep the extras in the fridge, and be that much closer to a quick lunch later in the week.

MAKES 2 SERVINGS

2 medium sweet potatoes
2 cups leftover tuna salad, Tex-Mex chicken, or Butter Chicken
½ cup shredded Cheddar cheese
1 cup shredded lettuce
2 tablespoons sour cream
1 green onion, thinly sliced

Preheat the oven to 425°F. Line a baking sheet with parchment paper or foil.

Pierce the sweet potatoes a few times with a fork and place on the prepared baking sheet. Roast for 40 to 45 minutes, until the skin puffs and the flesh is fork-tender. Allow the potatoes to cool for 5 to 10 minutes. Cut them end to end but not all the way through, then open with a fork to create a little pocket area where you can put your fillings.

If you're going with tuna, add the tuna cold, top with cheese, and pop in the oven on broil for 1 minute to allow the cheese to melt. Top with the lettuce, sour cream, and green onion.

If you're adding the chicken, heat it before putting it in the potatoes. Add the cheese, lettuce, sour cream, and green onion.

TUNA KEBABS

A few years ago, we were having lunch at the home of one of my good friends. Her mother-in-law was visiting from Pakistan and made these kebabs. Full of warming spices and savory tuna, they were so delicious and the kids just devoured them. Zee didn't even realize we were eating tuna, not meat! She was kind enough to share the recipe with me, and I have been making them ever since (and always send a little prayer her way when I do!). They're easy to make and store very well in the fridge for 4 to 5 days. You can serve them on their own, in a burger bun, or with a salad, such as the Bright Summer Kale Salad (page 114) or the Shirazi-Inspired Salad (page 105).

MAKES 10 TO 12 KEBABS

3 (5-ounce) cans water-packed tuna, drained
3 medium potatoes, cooked and mashed
½ small red onion, finely chopped
Handful of chopped cilantro
Juice of 1 lemon
1 green chile
1½ teaspoons garlic powder
Dash ground cinnamon
2 teaspoons ground cumin
1 teaspoon garam masala
3 tablespoons fried crispy onions (see Kitchen Staples, page 7)
1 teaspoon ground red chile
1 teaspoon red pepper flakes
1½ teaspoons salt
3 tablespoons canola or avocado oil

In a large bowl, mix all the ingredients except the oil until well incorporated, making sure the tuna is fully broken into small pieces. Feel free to use your hands and really mix everything well!

Form the tuna mixture into ten or twelve round kebabs (like a small burger patty, about ½ inch thick). Place on a parchment-lined baking sheet. (At this point, you can transfer the patties to an airtight container and store them in the freezer for up to a month. Thaw for about 30 minutes before cooking.)

Heat the oil in a frying pan over medium heat. Fry your kebabs until golden brown, for 3 to 4 minutes per side. Or to broil the kebabs, heat the oven on broil. Brush or spray the kebabs with oil and cook for 2 to 3 minutes per side or till they begin to get golden brown. Serve hot or at room temperature.

NOTE: While in English the word *kebab* means meat grilled on skewers, in the Middle East it can refer to meat cooked over flame, cut pieces of meat, or ground meat shaped into meatballs or patties. Kebabs can be made of lamb, beef, chicken, goat—or fish, as they are in this recipe!

BEEF KEBAB ROLLS

There's just something special about a perfectly spiced, juicy kebab. My family and friends are always so happy when they know I'm serving them up for lunch. I love that everyone can just grab some kebab and some naan and make their own wrap! And while they're a fantastic lunch option, they are also particularly popular with our family during Ramadan. For one month every year, Muslims fast during the daylight hours. We break our fast with Iftaar (a meal eaten after sunset), which frequently becomes a celebration.

I often prep these kebabs in advance and have them waiting in the freezer. Just pull them out about 30 minutes before you want to cook them.

MAKES 10 TO 12 KEBABS

BEEF KEBABS

2 small slices of bread (I use sprouted grain)
1 medium onion, cut in half
½ green chile, cut in half
1 bunch cilantro
1½ pounds ground beef
1 tablespoon garlic paste (page 13)
1 tablespoon ginger paste (page 13)
1½ teaspoons garam masala
1 teaspoon ground red chile
1 teaspoon salt
2 tablespoons neutral oil for pan-frying

FOR SERVING

10 naan (page 195), roti (page 192), or other flatbread
½ cup plain yogurt (optional)
1 tablespoon green chutney (page 14) (optional)
Ambli, for serving (optional)
Ketchup, for serving (optional)

In a food processor, pulse your pieces of bread until you have fine bread crumbs. Transfer them to a large bowl. Then place the onion, green chile, and cilantro in the food processor and pulse till they are well combined into very fine pieces, almost a paste. Add to the bread crumbs in the large bowl.

Add the ground beef, bread-crumb mixture, and the remaining ingredients except the oil to the bowl and mix everything until it's well combined. The best tools for this job are your (clean) hands!

Shape your meat mixture into ten to twelve small cylindrical kebabs, 4 to 5 inches in length. You could make the kebabs with or without a skewer. You can also freeze your kebabs at this point. Lay them flat on a baking tray and place in the freezer flat until they freeze, then you can transfer them to a container so they keep their shape and don't stick together. Take them out to thaw for 3 to 4 hours before you pan-fry or grill them.

Heat the oil in a frying pan over medium heat. Working in batches, add the kebabs and cook until browned and cooked through, for 2 to 3 minutes per side. Transfer the cooked kebabs to a plate.

If you'd like to serve the kebabs with a quick raita, stir together the yogurt and green chutney in a bowl.

Serve hot with the naan, raita, ambli, and/or ketchup.

PITA HUMMUS PIZZA

One summer day, I was staring hopefully into the fridge, looking for some lunch inspiration. We had some leftover cooked ground beef, and we always have pita and hummus—and from these everyday ingredients, an exceptional lunch was made! This pizza has since become a favorite in our house, especially since the kids can make it for themselves. It comes together superfast with no need to turn on the oven or stove (unless you need to cook some beef, but even that takes only a few minutes), and you'll love the sweet and savory combo with fresh pops of pomegranate in every bite.

MAKES 2 PIZZAS

2 large pita breads
3 tablespoons hummus
1 pound ground beef,
   cooked and crumbled
1½ cups microgreens,
   arugula, or spinach
2 tablespoons chopped
   cilantro
2 teaspoons sumac
2 tablespoons fresh lemon
   juice
2 teaspoons olive oil
½ cup pomegranate seeds

Warm your pitas in the microwave, toaster, or oven. Spread hummus over each pita. Top with ground beef, greens, and cilantro. Sprinkle with sumac, lemon juice, olive oil, and pomegranate seeds. Cut each pizza into quarters and enjoy!

BUTTER CHICKEN PIZZA

Out of all the recipes in this book, this is the one closest to my heart. It's something my son, Ahmed, and I created together. In our family, Ahmed's love for butter chicken is so well known—he is a self-proclaimed Butter Chicken expert!—that both my mother and mother-in-law frequently make it for him. Ahmed also loves pizza, so this fun twist on both those meals was the perfect pairing. We make these all the time for friends and family, and they're always a hit. You'll love how the rich, savory curry flavor of the butter chicken pairs with the traditional pizza toppings of tomato sauce and cheese. And with premade naan as your crust, these pizzas come together in a snap! Top them with cilantro for a fresh and herbaceous finish and green chiles for some heat.

MAKES 4 NAAN PIZZAS OR 12 MINI PIZZAS

- 2 cups Butter Chicken (page 158; cut the chicken into very small pieces)
- ¼ cup pizza sauce
- 4 large naan or 12 mini naan
- 2 cups shredded mozzarella cheese
- ½ medium red onion, thinly sliced
- 1-2 small green chiles, thinly sliced (optional)
- ¼ cup chopped cilantro
- Handful of microgreens, for topping (optional)

Preheat the oven to 375°F. Line a large rimmed baking sheet with parchment paper.

Combine the Butter Chicken and pizza sauce in a medium saucepan and bring to a simmer over medium heat.

Arrange the naan on the prepared baking sheet. Top each with some of the butter chicken sauce and then mozzarella, onion, and green chiles, if using.

Bake for 8 to 10 minutes until the cheese melts. Optionally, you can broil them for 1 minute at the end of cooking time until the cheese turns golden brown.

Top with the cilantro and microgreens, if using. Cut into slices and serve hot.

TEX-MEX SHREDDED CHICKEN TACOS

Like the chicken in my Spicy Soy Chicken Lettuce Wraps (page 77), this Tex-Mex shredded chicken is a great staple you can make on Sunday or Monday (or any other day!) and use to create different dishes for the rest of the week. The shredded chicken works great with tortillas and taco fixings. If you've got leftovers, use it to top nachos, throw in a soup, or add to a salad for some extra protein.

MAKES 12 TACOS

TEX-MEX SHREDDED CHICKEN

1 cup crushed tomatoes
3–4 large chipotle peppers in adobo sauce, cut in half
2 garlic cloves, minced
2 packets fajita or taco seasoning
1 tablespoon ground cumin
1 teaspoon chili powder
2 tablespoons salsa
Juice of ½ lime
4 large boneless, skinless chicken breasts

WRAPS

12 (6-inch) flour tortillas or tortilla cups (see Note)

OPTIONAL TOPPINGS

Guacamole (page 188 or store-bought)
Sour cream
Grated Cheddar cheese
Shredded lettuce
Chopped jalapeños
Chopped chipotle peppers

Select the SAUTÉ mode on an Instant Pot. Put in the crushed tomatoes, chipotles, garlic, seasoning mix, cumin, chili powder, salsa, and lime juice. Cook until the sauce begins to simmer, for 4 to 5 minutes. Add the chicken breasts and turn to coat them in the sauce.

Press CANCEL. Lock the lid into place and set to sealing. Cook on high pressure for 20 minutes, then turn the Instant Pot to low and cook 10 minutes more. Release the pressure naturally for 10 minutes, then manually release the remaining pressure, press CANCEL, and remove the lid.

Remove the chicken from the Instant Pot and set aside in a bowl. Blend the sauce with an immersion blender until smooth.

Shred the chicken using two forks to pull the meat into small pieces and then put it back in the pot with the sauce. Stir to incorporate.

Serve the chicken on tortillas with your toppings of choice.

Store any leftover chicken in an airtight container in the fridge for up to 5 days.

NOTE: To make the tortilla cups, heat the oven to 200°F. Heat the tortillas in the microwave for 15 to 20 seconds so they are warm and easy to shape. Spray the back of a muffin tray with oil and mold the tortilla to the bottom of the muffin tray that's been placed upside down. Cook in the oven for 16 to 20 minutes, until the tortillas have hardened and crisp up and hold the shape of a cup. Remove from the oven and allow the cups to cool till they are easy to handle.

CRUNCHY TORTILLA WRAPS

I love re-creating fun meals we find in restaurants and fast-food chains and giving them healthier twists—but making sure they're every bit as delicious as the restaurant versions (to keep the kids excited to eat them). These crunchy tortilla wraps are a perfect example of that. The crunch is added by sneaking in a few spicy Doritos! I love the mix of the salty, crunchy Doritos with the freshness of crisp lettuce and tomatoes along with the creamy chicken, sour cream, and avocado. And the chicken is the same one we used for the Tex-Mex tacos on page 74, so if you have that on hand already, these are super easy to make for a quick lunch.

MAKES 4 WRAPS

8 flour tortillas, 4 large and 4 small
¼ cup sour cream
¼ cup guacamole (page 188 or store-bought) (optional)
1 cup shredded Cheddar cheese
2 cups Tex-Mex Shredded Chicken (page 74)
1 cup shredded lettuce
1 large tomato, diced
16–20 seasoned tortilla chips, such as Doritos
1–2 tablespoons mayonnaise
Hot sauce, for serving
Lime wedges, for serving

To make each wrap: Place a large tortilla on your work surface. Spread it with 1 tablespoon of the sour cream and 1 tablespoon of guacamole (if using), then top with some of the cheese, ½ cup of shredded chicken, lettuce, and tomatoes. Place four to five chips on top and cover with a small tortilla, pressing everything down. Brush the top of the small tortilla with a little mayo and fold the edges of the large bottom tortilla over the small tortilla to close the wrap. Repeat with the remaining ingredients to make the other three wraps.

Heat a frying pan over medium heat. Carefully transfer one of the wraps to the pan, folded side down. Brush the large tortilla with mayonnaise. Cook for 2 to 3 minutes until browned and crisp underneath, then flip and cook for 2 to 3 minutes more.

Repeat the same process for each tortilla.

Serve with hot sauce and lime.

SPICY SOY CHICKEN LETTUCE WRAPS

These easy lettuce wraps come together quickly thanks to chicken cooked in your Instant Pot or pressure cooker. For extra convenience, the chicken can be made ahead and stored in the fridge for up to a week, so you can assemble your lettuce wraps as you need them. But don't sleep on the other possibilities for the shredded chicken; it can be added to so many dishes, like salads, pastas, and fried rice, all week long.

MAKES 10 TO 12 LETTUCE WRAPS

SPICY SOY CHICKEN

3 large boneless, skinless chicken breasts

1 tablespoon garlic paste (page 13)

1 tablespoon ginger paste (page 13)

1½ tablespoons soy sauce

2 teaspoons chile sauce, such as Sriracha

1 teaspoon ground black pepper

1 cup water

WRAPS

10 whole lettuce leaves

1 large carrot, shredded

½ red bell pepper, cut into very thin strips

2 green onions, chopped

1 tablespoon black sesame seeds

Place the chicken and all the marinade ingredients in an Instant Pot and give it all a stir. Lock the lid into place and set to sealing. Cook for 12 minutes on high pressure.

Release the pressure naturally for 10 minutes, then manually release the remaining pressure, press CANCEL, and remove the lid. Shred the chicken using two forks to pull the meat into small pieces. (At this point, you can proceed with the recipe or transfer the chicken to an airtight container and store in the fridge for up to 1 week. The chicken can be used hot or cold.)

To make a wrap, put some chicken on a lettuce leaf and top with some of the shredded carrot, pepper, green onion, and a sprinkle of sesame seeds. Repeat with remaining ingredients. Serve right away.

HEALTHY CHAAT

Chaat describes a whole category of Indian street foods. There are many varieties, but all of them combine sweet, spicy, tangy, and crunchy ingredients to make a party for your palate! Chaat often involves fried components. This healthier version is a light meal of chickpeas and potatoes, topped with lots of fresh veggies and delicious spices, served cold with a sweet and spicy yogurt sauce. It looks so beautiful with all its layers, making it a perfect lunch to serve for guests. With just a little prep and not much cooking, you can make it in the morning and allow it to sit for a few hours; the flavors only get better over time!

MAKES 8 SERVINGS

CHAAT
2 large potatoes
1 (15-ounce) can chickpeas, drained and rinsed
1 tablespoon lemon juice
½ teaspoon chaat masala powder, plus more for garnish (see Tips)
¼ teaspoon ground cumin
½ teaspoon ground red chile
¼ teaspoon salt
¼ teaspoon ground black pepper
½ cup finely chopped onion
½ cup finely chopped tomato
¼ cup chopped cilantro, plus more for garnish
1 green chile, chopped
1 cup ambli
½ cup green chutney (page 14)
Pani puri (see Tips), crushed

Bring a large pot of water to boil. Add the whole potatoes and cook until fork-tender, about 20 minutes (stick a knife into the center to check for doneness). Remove the potatoes from the boiling water and let them cool to room temperature. Peel the potatoes and cut them into small cubes, then transfer to a serving bowl.

While the potatoes are boiling, in a large bowl, stir together the ingredients for the Sweet and Spicy Yogurt.

To the bowl with the potatoes, add the chickpeas, lemon juice, chaat masala, cumin, ground red chile, and salt and pepper and toss to combine. Add the onion, tomato, cilantro, and green chile and stir to incorporate. Layer the yogurt over the vegetable mixture. Drizzle with ambli and green chutney and sprinkle with a little extra chaat masala and cilantro. Serve at room temperature or even straight out of the fridge with the crushed Pani puri sprinkled on top!

SWEET AND SPICY YOGURT

2 cups plain yogurt
1 teaspoon sugar
¼ teaspoon ground red chile
¼ teaspoon ground cumin
½ teaspoon chaat masala powder
½ teaspoon salt

TIPS: Chaat masala is a spice blend that gives chaat its distinctive taste. It is made with Himalayan black salt, or kala namak, which gives a savory flavor and egg-like aroma to your chaat. Pani puri are spicy, crunchy snacks sold flat. You can find both these ingredients at Asian grocery stores or online.

CHANA BATETA
(Chickpea and Potato Curry)

This vegetarian curry is a staple at my parents' house. If I tell my mom we're coming over, she'll whip this up so it's ready for us to sit down and enjoy when we arrive. It's served up like a soup, with a spicy tomato sauce that complements the hearty potatoes and chickpeas. But for me, the best part is all the toppings that go along with it, like chevro (an East African savory snack), mung bean fritters, chips, coconut chutney, and ambli.

MAKES 4 TO 6
SERVINGS

CURRY

1 large potato, peeled and
    cut into ½-inch chunks
1 teaspoon salt
¼ cup ambli
1 tablespoon tomato paste
1 teaspoon ground turmeric
½ teaspoon ground red chile
1 teaspoon gram flour
    (chickpea flour)
½ teaspoon brown sugar
2 tablespoons lemon juice
    (optional)
3 tablespoons canola oil
5 curry leaves
¼ teaspoon black mustard
    seeds
¼ teaspoon cumin seeds
1 dried red chile or fresh
    green chile (optional)
½ teaspoon garlic paste
    (page 13)
1 (19-ounce) can of
    chickpeas, drained

TOPPINGS

Bhajia (Mung Bean Fritters)
    (page 201)
Coconut chutney (page 16)
Ambli
Chevro (see Tip) or plain
    potato chips

Bring a large pot of water to a boil. Add the potatoes and a pinch of salt and cook the potatoes until fork-tender, for 10 to 12 minutes. Drain the potatoes, retaining 2 cups of the cooking water.

In a bowl, stir together the ambli, tomato paste, turmeric, salt, ground red chile, gram flour, brown sugar, and lemon juice (if using) and set aside.

In a large pot, heat the oil on medium-high heat. Add the curry leaves, mustard seeds, cumin seeds, and dried chile (if using) and toast for about a minute, until the ingredients become fragrant. Add the garlic paste and cook for 30 seconds, then stir in the ambli mixture and cook for 2 to 3 minutes, until it begins to thicken.

Add the cooked potatoes and chickpeas, along with the reserved cooking water. Give everything a stir. Add another cup of water to make more gravy. Bring the mixture to a boil, then cook for 3 to 5 minutes. The curry is ready when you see the oil separate at the top.

Ladle the curry into bowls. Place all your toppings in bowls on the table so people can help themselves.

TIP: Chevro (sometimes spelled chevdo or chevda) is a savory snack mix of rice puffs mixed with nuts and chickpeas. You can find it in most South Asian grocery stores or online.

BAKED CHICKEN NUGGETS

When our kids started having playdates, I wanted to offer Ahmed, Asiyah, and their friends something healthy, but also something they'd be happy to see on the table. Enter these chicken nuggets. The delicious coating gives them a great crunch, and the slightly spicy sauce is downright irresistible. We may be growing out of the playdate stage, but these nuggets are here to stay.

MAKES 12 TO 15 NUGGETS

NUGGETS

2 eggs
1 tablespoon milk
3 teaspoons garlic powder
3 teaspoons smoked paprika
2½ teaspoons salt
1 teaspoon ground black pepper
1 cup almond or oat flour
½ cup bread crumbs
2 tablespoons chopped cilantro or parsley
4 medium-sized boneless, skinless chicken breasts (about 1½ pounds), cut in 1½-inch cubes

DIPPING SAUCE

⅓ cup mayo
2 teaspoons ketchup
1 teaspoon mustard
1 teaspoon Sriracha sauce

Preheat the oven to 425°F. Line a rimmed baking sheet with parchment paper.

Prepare your dredging stations! In one shallow bowl, whisk the eggs and milk with 1½ teaspoons of the garlic powder, 1½ teaspoons of the paprika, 1 teaspoon of the salt, and the pepper. In another shallow bowl, combine your flour, bread crumbs, and cilantro with the remaining 1½ teaspoons garlic powder, 1½ teaspoons paprika, and 1½ teaspoons salt.

Dip a piece of chicken in the egg mixture, then dredge it through the crumb mix to completely coat the nugget and place it on your prepared baking sheet. Repeat with all the chicken pieces.

Bake for 8 to 10 minutes, then flip the nuggets and bake for another 5 to 6 minutes until the chicken is golden brown and cooked through. Cut into a piece to be sure!

While the nuggets bake, combine your dipping sauce ingredients in a bowl and stir well.

Serve the nuggets with the dipping sauce.

SOUPS

WHO DOESN'T LOVE A GOOD SOUP? MOST SOUP recipes are easy, they're a great way to add nutrition into your meals, they can be made in advance and kept in the freezer to bail you out on some future mealtime, and the varieties from around the world are endless. But soup's best feature is its nourishing, nurturing quality. There's something so reassuring and satisfying about a warm serving of love in a bowl.

CURRIED CITRUS LENTIL SOUP

I first tried this hearty yet bright soup while my family and I were visiting Morocco. I think we went back to the same restaurant three times in the five days we were in Marrakech! Each time we were there, I'd ask them about the recipe and slowly teased out all the ingredients. What makes this soup unique is all the citrus juice, which is cooked with the spices to intensify their flavors. I make this soup all the time, and it's just as delicious with chicken as it is when made completely vegetarian. It also freezes and reheats beautifully.

MAKES 6 SERVINGS

1 cup dried red lentils
1 tablespoon olive oil
1 medium onion, diced
2 medium carrots, diced
2 celery stalks, diced
3 garlic cloves, minced
2 tablespoons grated fresh
   ginger
1 teaspoon curry powder
1 teaspoon ground cumin
1 teaspoon ground
   coriander
Juice of 1 lemon, plus more
   for serving
Juice of 2 limes
1 bay leaf
2 chicken drumsticks
   (optional)
10 cups chicken or vegetable
   stock
Salt and pepper to taste
½ cup chopped cilantro,
   plus more for serving
Plain yogurt or sour cream,
   for serving (optional)

Pour the lentils into a large bowl and cover with cold water by 1 inch. Soak for 15 to 20 minutes.

Heat the oil in a large pot over medium heat. Add the onion, carrots, and celery and cook for 7 to 10 minutes, or until they start to become soft. Add the garlic, ginger, curry, cumin, and coriander and cook, stirring, for 45 seconds or until fragrant. Add the lemon and lime juice and give everything a good stir; cook for 1 to 2 minutes to intensify the flavors. Drain the lentils and add them to the pot along with the bay leaf, chicken drumsticks (if using), and stock.

Increase the heat to medium-high and cook till the soup begins to boil, then cover and simmer until the lentils are softened and the chicken is cooked through, 45 to 55 minutes. Remove and discard the bay leaf. Remove the chicken and shred the meat off the bones, then stir the shredded chicken back into the soup. Season with salt and pepper to taste. Remove the pot from the heat and add the cilantro.

Ladle the soup into bowls. Serve with a dollop of yogurt, cilantro, and lemon.

This soup will keep in the fridge for 5 days and freezes really well.

CREAMY COCONUT LENTIL SOUP

This creamy lentil soup is a meal on its own—cozy enough for a Sunday lunch but complex enough to serve for a dinner party with the richness of the coconut milk, the kick of spice, and the bright pop of lemon juice. I love the way the house smells when I cook it. And so does my family, judging by the way they come wandering into the kitchen when they smell this soup simmering away on the stove.

MAKES 6 SERVINGS

1½ cups dried red lentils
1 tablespoon coconut or olive oil
1 large onion, chopped
3 garlic cloves, minced
2 tablespoons minced fresh ginger
2 tablespoons tomato paste
1 tablespoon curry powder
½ teaspoon red pepper flakes
1 tomato, chopped
5 cups chicken or vegetable stock
1 (13.5-ounce) can coconut milk
2–3 handfuls kale or spinach, chopped
Juice of ½ lemon
Salt and pepper to taste
Chopped cilantro, for garnish

Pour the lentils into a bowl and cover with cold water by 1 inch. Soak for 15 to 20 minutes, then drain.

In a stockpot, heat the oil over medium heat. Add the onion, garlic, and ginger and cook until the onion is translucent, for 4 to 5 minutes. Add the tomato paste, curry powder, and red pepper flakes and cook, stirring, for another minute. Add the chopped tomato and cook until the pieces begin to break down and soften. Add the stock, coconut milk, and lentils. Bring to a boil, then cover and simmer until the lentils are very tender, for 20 to 30 minutes. If you would like a creamier consistency, blend the soup until smooth, either with an immersion blender or in batches in a conventional blender, then return the soup to the pot.

Stir in the kale and lemon juice and cook until the greens are slightly wilted, for 2 to 3 minutes. Season with salt and pepper to taste.

Ladle the soup into bowls and serve topped with cilantro.

This soup will keep in the fridge for 5 days and freezes really well.

MUNG BEAN SOUP

My dad is a soup guy! Every day for as long as I can remember, he has had some kind of soup. This mung bean soup is the kind of simple, delicious soup my mom would cook in a big batch and store in the freezer, so there was always some waiting for Dad to just warm it up. It's full of spice and completely vegetarian.

MAKES 6 SERVINGS

1 cup dried mung beans
2 tablespoons olive oil
1 medium onion, finely
   chopped
1 teaspoon garlic paste
   (page 13)
1 teaspoon ginger paste
   (page 13)
2 medium tomatoes,
   chopped
1 teaspoon ground red chile
1 teaspoon ground turmeric
1 teaspoon ground cumin
1 teaspoon ground
   coriander
1 tablespoon fenugreek
   leaves (mehthi)
Salt and pepper to taste
Cilantro and lemon wedges,
   for garnish

Place the mung beans in a large bowl and cover them with cold water. Allow them to soak for a few hours. Pour the mung beans into a mesh strainer and rinse well with cold water.

Bring 3 cups of water to a boil in a large pot and add the beans. Lower the heat to a simmer and cook for about 30 minutes, until the beans are soft. Drain the beans and set aside.

In a large pot, heat the oil over medium heat and add the onion, garlic paste, and ginger paste. Cook until the onion begins to soften and the garlic and ginger become fragrant, for 2 to 3 minutes. Add the tomatoes and cook until they begin to break down into a sauce-like consistency. Add the ground red chile, turmeric, cumin, and coriander and mix well. Stir in about ¼ cup of water to make a nice, thick sauce. Add the fenugreek leaves and salt and pepper to taste and mix well.

Add the mung beans to the sauce and stir to combine. Add 3 cups water and bring the soup to a simmer. Cook for about 7 minutes until the flavors come together and the soup is your desired consistency.

Top with cilantro and lemon juice.

This soup will keep in the fridge for 5 days and freezes really well.

HEARTY CABBAGE SOUP

Vegetable soup is usually associated with the spring; this one is a hearty, veggie-packed soup that is ideal for a cold fall or winter night. I love making it in an Instant Pot because you can just set it and forget it. If you don't have one, you can absolutely make this in a large pot on the stove.

MAKES 8 SERVINGS

3 tablespoons olive oil
1 medium onion, chopped
3 garlic cloves, minced
1 teaspoon grated fresh ginger
2 medium carrots, chopped
2 celery stalks, chopped
1 large zucchini, chopped
2 medium potatoes, chopped
2 teaspoons dried thyme
1 teaspoon dried rosemary
2 bay leaves
1 tablespoon Italian seasoning
3 teaspoons salt
2 teaspoons ground black pepper
8 cups stock (veggie or chicken)
1 medium tomato, diced
1 cup strained tomatoes
3–4 cups cabbage, chopped
Chopped parsley, for garnish

Stovetop: Heat the olive oil in a large pot over medium-high heat. Add the onion, garlic, and ginger and cook until fragrant, for 2 to 3 minutes. Add the carrots, celery, and zucchini and stir to combine for 5 minutes, till the vegetables begin to soften. Add the potatoes and all the seasonings (thyme, rosemary, bay leaves, Italian seasoning, salt, and pepper). Mix well to coat the potatoes with the seasonings. Allow the potatoes to cook for 2 to 3 minutes. Finally pour in the stock, tomatoes, strained tomatoes, and cabbage. Mix well to combine.

Bring the soup to a boil, then cover and simmer until the vegetables are tender, for 45 minutes. Remove the bay leaves and adjust the seasonings to taste.

Ladle the soup into bowls and top with the parsley.

Instant Pot: If cooking in the Instant Pot, heat the oil using the SAUTÉ mode. Add the ingredients and cook as noted above; press CANCEL. Lock the lid into place and set to sealing. Cook on high pressure for 15 minutes. Release the pressure naturally for 15 minutes, then manually release the remaining pressure, press CANCEL, and remove the lid.

Remove the bay leaves and adjust the seasonings to taste. Ladle the soup into bowls and top with the parsley.

This soup will keep in the fridge for 5 days and freezes really well.

ROASTED BUTTERNUT SQUASH AND BEET SOUP

Do you ever make something just because the color is so beautiful? This soup has the most gorgeous pink hue. Living in Canada, we love to celebrate the changing seasons with food, and this is a great way to kick off autumn. It will fill your kitchen with all the fragrance of fall. Roasting the squash, beets, onions, and garlic adds such a depth of flavor—and the oven does most of the work for you. For a satisfying meal, serve with crusty bread or grilled cheese sandwiches.

MAKES 6 SERVINGS

1 medium butternut squash, peeled and cut into 1-inch chunks
3 beets, peeled and cut into 1-inch chunks
1 large onion, roughly chopped
1 head of garlic, sliced in half crosswise
1½ tablespoons olive oil
2 tablespoons butter, cubed
2–3 thyme sprigs
Salt and pepper to taste
2 cups chicken or vegetable stock
¾ cup coconut milk, plus more for garnish
Pumpkin seeds, for garnish (optional)

Preheat the oven to 350°F.

Place all the vegetables on a rimmed baking dish and toss with the olive oil, butter cubes, thyme, and salt and pepper to taste. If you place your garlic bulb halves cut side up, they're less likely to burn. Roast until all the veggies are fork-tender, for 45 to 50 minutes. Let everything cool on the tray until you can comfortably handle the veggies.

Put the onions, squash, and beets in a blender. Squeeze the roasted garlic cloves into the blender (discard the skins). Add the stock and coconut milk and blend well until your soup is very smooth; you may need to work in batches if your blender isn't big enough. Season to taste with salt and pepper. You can serve it from the blender, but I like to transfer the soup to a large pot and let it simmer for another 15 minutes before serving.

Ladle the soup into bowls and top with extra coconut milk and pumpkin seeds, if desired.

This soup will keep in the fridge for 5 days and freezes really well.

ROASTED TOMATO SOUP WITH GRILLED CHEESE

At brunch on a trip to San Francisco, the kids ordered grilled cheese and it came with tomato soup. The kids and Zee fell in love with it and urged me to try some. Based on my childhood memories, I initially resisted—growing up, I only ever had the canned kind, and so I thought tomato soup was nothing special—but when I had a spoonful at their urging, I was blown away (I ended up ordering a whole bowl for myself!). As soon as we got home, I got to work re-creating it. My version of the soup gets a depth of flavor from balsamic vinegar and some creaminess (without dairy!) from cashews.

MAKES 8 SERVINGS

SOUP
10–12 large roma tomatoes, cut in half
2 garlic bulbs, sliced in half
3 tablespoons olive oil
1 tablespoon balsamic vinegar
½ teaspoon dried oregano
Salt and pepper to taste
1 large red onion, sliced
4 cups vegetable stock
½ cup cashews
½ teaspoon dried basil
1 tablespoon tomato paste
1 teaspoon red pepper flakes
½ cup fresh basil leaves, for garnish
Grated Parmesan cheese, for garnish (optional)

GRILLED CHEESE
4 slices of bread (white, whole wheat, or rye)
4–6 slices of cheese (Cheddar, American, Swiss, or any melting cheese of your choice)
Butter, softened

Preheat the oven to 400°F.

Arrange the tomatoes and garlic in a large rimmed baking dish. Drizzle with 1½ tablespoons of the olive oil and the balsamic vinegar, then sprinkle with oregano, and salt and pepper to taste. Toss to coat. Make sure the garlic bulbs are cut side up, then roast until the tomatoes soften and begin to break down, for 35 to 40 minutes.

While the tomatoes and garlic are roasting, heat the remaining 1½ tablespoons olive oil in a large pot over low heat. Add the onion and brown, stirring occasionally, until caramelized, about 20 minutes.

Squeeze the roasted garlic cloves into the pot (discard the skins) and add the cooked tomatoes. Stir in the stock, cashews, basil, tomato paste, and red pepper flakes. Bring the soup to a simmer and cook for 20 minutes until the cashews are very soft. Purée in the pot with an immersion blender or in a stand blender (you may need to work in batches).

While the soup simmers, make the grilled cheese.

Preheat a nonstick skillet or griddle over medium heat.

Take two slices of bread and spread a thin layer of butter on one side of each slice.

Place one slice of bread, buttered side down, onto the heated skillet. Layer the cheese slices evenly on top of the bread. Once the cheese begins to melt slightly, about 2 minutes, take the second slice of bread, buttered side up, and place it on top of the cheese. Cook the sandwich for 2 to 3 minutes on each side, or until the bread turns golden brown and the cheese starts to melt. You can

press the sandwich gently to help the cheese melt evenly—for me, the cheesier the better.

Once the sandwich is cooked to your level of crispiness, remove it from the skillet and place it on a cutting board or plate. Let it cool for a minute or two to avoid burning your mouth.

Cut the grilled cheese sandwich in half or even long strips, which is great for dipping into your soup.

Divide the soup between bowls and top with fresh basil and Parmesan cheese, if desired. Serve with the grilled cheese sandwiches.

This soup will keep in the fridge for 3 days and freezes really well.

CHICKEN CORN SOUP

The beauty of this rich and comforting soup is that you create a flavorful broth at the same time that the rest of the soup is cooking. It's really simple to whip up since everything just goes in one pot, and it makes a great lunch or dinner on a chilly day.

MAKES 6 SERVINGS

3 tablespoons olive oil
4 skinless, bone-in chicken thighs
2 tablespoons garlic paste (page 13)
1 tablespoon ginger paste (page 13)
1½ teaspoons ground black pepper
1 teaspoon salt
1 large onion, chopped
6 cups water or chicken stock
1 handful cilantro stems
2 cups cooked corn (canned or frozen)
2 tablespoons soy sauce
1 tablespoon cornstarch
⅓ cup chopped cilantro
¼ cup chopped green onions

Heat 2 tablespoons of the olive oil in a large pot over medium-high heat. Add the chicken thighs, garlic paste, ginger paste, pepper, and salt. Give it all a good stir. Cook until the chicken has browned, for 2 to 3 minutes per side. Remove the chicken from the pot and set aside on a plate.

Add the remaining 1 tablespoon olive oil and onion to the pot, and cook until the onion begins to brown.

Put the chicken back in the pot, along with any juices that have accumulated. Pour in the water and bring to a boil. Add the cilantro stems, then simmer until the chicken is cooked through, for 25 to 30 minutes.

Remove the chicken from the soup and set it aside on a clean plate. When it's cool enough to handle, shred the meat off the bones. Remove and discard the cilantro stems.

Add the corn, soy sauce, and shredded chicken to the pot and simmer for 10 minutes to let the flavors meld.

Make a slurry by combining the cornstarch with 3 tablespoons cold water in a small bowl. Stir the slurry into the soup to thicken it.

If you like, purée the soup with an immersion blender until it reaches your desired consistency. I like it blended slightly so you can still get whole corn kernels and large pieces of shredded chicken.

Taste the soup and add salt and pepper to taste. Ladle the soup into bowls and serve topped with the cilantro and green onion.

This soup will keep in the fridge for 3 days and freezes really well.

EAST ASIAN-INSPIRED CHICKEN AND VEGGIE SOUP

I'm always testing the limits on how many veggies I can add to recipes before my family is onto me. This shredded chicken and veggie soup came about when I was trying to finish up a bunch of veggies from the fridge, and it was a hit—so much so that it's made it into our regular recipe rotation. It's easy to throw together if you have some leftover cooked chicken on hand. You can play around with the heat level by adding more or less Sriracha and make it subtle or more spicy (sometimes I like it when the pepper hits you in the face, but I kept it medium spicy here!). Also, if you don't have both regular and dark soy sauce, just double up the regular soy sauce.

This soup gets a fresh flavor from a whole bunch of cilantro. Wash the bunch well to remove grit and keep it bundled together (if your cilantro bunch has the root attached, leave it on!). That way, you can easily remove the stems before serving.

MAKES 8 SERVINGS

2 tablespoons sesame oil
1 large white onion, thinly sliced
2 garlic cloves, minced
1-inch piece of ginger, grated
2 large carrots, thinly sliced
1 large red bell pepper, thinly sliced
2 tablespoons oyster sauce
1 tablespoon soy sauce
1 tablespoon dark soy sauce
2 teaspoons Sriracha or other chile sauce
1½ cups cooked shredded chicken
1½ cups frozen corn
1 large bunch cilantro
7 cups chicken stock
2 cups shredded red cabbage
¼ cup green onions, thinly sliced for garnish

In a large pot, heat the sesame oil over medium heat. Add the onion, garlic, and ginger and cook, stirring occasionally, until fragrant, for 2 to 3 minutes. Add the carrot and red pepper and cook for another 3 to 4 minutes.

Add the oyster sauce, soy sauces, and Sriracha and give it all a stir. Add the chicken and corn. Tear off a small handful of cilantro leaves, set them aside, and put the remaining bunch in the pot.

Cover the soup with chicken stock, then simmer for 5 minutes. Add the cabbage and simmer for another 8 to 10 minutes until the veggies are cooked but still have a little bite.

Remove the bunch of cilantro and discard. Ladle the soup into large bowls and top with the reserved cilantro leaves and green onions.

This soup will keep in the fridge for 5 days and freezes really well.

FEEL GOOD CHICKEN NOODLE SOUP

Chicken noodle soup is truly a cure-all. Whether you've got a kid with a scratchy throat or you're the one who is having a rough week, chicken soup is good for the body and the soul. This version is packed with healthy veggies, tender chicken, and soft chewy egg noodles (my family loves to slurp them up!). It gets a little something special from the ginger too, which can help alleviate any sniffles or upset stomachs and also adds some aromatic flavor to the broth.

MAKES 8 SERVINGS

2 tablespoons olive oil

4 boneless, skinless chicken thighs

3 teaspoons salt (2 teaspoons for the chicken, 1 for the soup)

3 teaspoons ground black pepper (2 teaspoons for the chicken, 1 for the soup)

3 celery stalks, chopped

1 large onion, diced

1 large carrot, chopped

1 zucchini, chopped

4 garlic cloves, minced

1 tablespoon chopped ginger

8 cups chicken stock

2 bay leaves

3 cups egg noodles

¼ cup chopped cilantro or parsley

1 tablespoon fresh lemon juice

In a large pot, heat the olive oil over medium heat. Season the chicken thighs with 2 teaspoons each of salt and pepper and then place them in the pot. Cook until lightly browned, for 3 to 4 minutes on each side. Remove the chicken from the pot and set aside on a plate.

Add the celery, onion, carrot, and zucchini to the pot and cook until the vegetables begin to soften, about 2 minutes, then add the garlic and ginger. Give everything a stir. Add the stock and bay leaves and season with the remaining teaspoon each of salt and pepper.

Bring the soup to a boil, then add the chicken thighs back in, cover, and simmer for 30 minutes until the vegetables are tender.

Remove the cooked chicken from the soup and set it on a clean plate. When cool enough to handle, shred the chicken into small pieces.

Add the noodles to the soup and cook for 8 to 10 minutes. Add the shredded chicken and mix until heated through.

Finish the soup with cilantro and lemon juice and ladle into bowls.

This soup will keep in the fridge for 3 days and freezes really well.

CHICKEN ENCHILADA SOUP

I love me a good soup, but sometimes I admit it's more about the toppings, like with this rich and creamy enchilada soup that you can load up with jalapeños, avocado, lime, cilantro, sharp shredded cheese, and tortilla chips. I like to put all the extras on the table and let my family choose what they're in the mood for that night. It's a party in a bowl! Best of all, it comes together quickly thanks to some smart shortcuts: I use low-salt store-bought taco seasoning for flavor as well as precooked chicken, and it's all cooked in the Instant Pot to save even more time. Make a double batch and enjoy it all week.

MAKES 6 TO 8 SERVINGS

1 tablespoon olive oil
2 medium onions, chopped
1 bell pepper (red, orange, or yellow), chopped
4 garlic cloves, chopped
2 tablespoons taco or fajita seasoning
2 tablespoons ground cumin
1 tablespoon smoked paprika
1 teaspoon salt
1 (15-ounce) can fire-roasted tomatoes
1 tablespoon tomato paste
5 cups chicken or vegetable stock or water
1 (15-ounce) can black beans, drained and rinsed
1 (15-ounce) can kidney beans, drained and rinsed
1 (15-ounce) can sweet corn, drained
2 cups shredded chicken (see Tex-Mex Shredded Chicken, page 74)

FOR THE TOPPINGS
Sliced jalapeños
Avocado
Shredded cheese
Sour cream
Chopped cilantro
Tortilla chips
Lime wedges

Heat the olive oil in a large pot. Add the onions, pepper, and garlic and sauté until they begin to soften, for 2 to 3 minutes. Add the spices and mix well. Stir in the tomatoes and tomato paste and cook until they begin to soften, about 5 minutes. Pour in the stock.

Allow the soup to come to a boil, then simmer. Place a lid on the pot and cook for about 15 minutes.

Remove the lid and blend the soup until smooth with an immersion blender or in a regular blender (you may need to work in batches). Add the beans, corn, and chicken and stir well. Bring the soup to a simmer and it's ready to serve. Ladle into bowls and top with all your favorite toppings!

This soup will keep in the fridge for a week and freezes really well.

SHURBO
(Meat and Grain Soup)

Shurbo is a filling meat and grain soup that's usually made with cracked wheat and takes hours to cook. It's traditionally made when someone is sick, has just given birth, or is recovering from an injury, and it's also a staple in many households during Ramadan. Think bone broth with added nutrients and spice! Substituting oats for the cracked wheat makes the cooking time so much faster and still gives you the hearty nutritional benefits. This shurbo is a delicious creamy soup with shredded beef that is perfect for cold days. I like to serve it with naan on the side for dipping.

MAKES 8 SERVINGS

1 pound boneless meat, stew pieces
1 tablespoon garlic paste (page 13)
1 tablespoon ginger paste (page 13)
4 teaspoons salt
2 teaspoons ground black pepper
6 cups water
1 tablespoon neutral oil, such as avocado or canola
1 onion, finely chopped
1 tomato, grated or chopped finely
2 teaspoons garam masala
1 teaspoon ground turmeric
1 green chile, finely chopped (optional)
½ cup quick oats or wheat germ
2 tablespoons chopped cilantro
Juice of 1 lemon
Sliced hot pepper, for garnish (optional)
Julienned fresh ginger, for garnish (optional)

In a large stockpot, cover the meat, garlic paste, ginger paste, 2 teaspoons of the salt, and 1 teaspoon of the pepper with the water. Bring to a boil, then simmer for 40 minutes, or until the meat is completely tender. Remove the meat from the stock, shred it, and set aside. Keep the cooking liquid; that is the flavorful broth you will use for the shurbo.

In a separate pot, heat the oil over medium heat. Add the onion and fry until translucent, for 5 minutes. Add the tomato, garam masala, turmeric, chile (if using), 2 teaspoons salt, and 1 teaspoon pepper and mix well. Cook until the tomato breaks down and the sauce thickens slightly. Then add 4 to 6 cups of the meat stock. If you don't have enough liquid, just top up the rest with water. Bring the soup to a boil. Add the oats and stir well. Simmer for 25 minutes until the soup has thickened slightly, stirring occasionally so the oats don't stick to the bottom. If you find it thickening too much, just add a little more water.

Stir in the meat and mix well; let it cook just until the meat is heated through. Ladle the soup into bowls. Top with cilantro, lemon juice, and optional sliced peppers and ginger.

This soup will keep in the fridge for 3 days and freezes really well.

SALADS

WHENEVER WE'RE INVITED ANYWHERE FOR
a potluck or meal, I'm always the person responsible
for bringing salad because I love it. A crisp and crunchy
salad can lighten up an otherwise rich meal, and
one with grains or pasta along with veggies can be
a meal unto itself. Above all, salad is a brilliant vehicle
for flavors of all kinds—from bright citrus to fresh
herbs and sharp cheeses. I like to serve (and eat!)
a salad every day.

SHIRAZI-INSPIRED SALAD

Shirazi, a delightful and refreshing Iranian salad, combines the vibrant flavors of tomatoes, cucumbers, onions, and herbs. Traditionally, it is dressed with sour grape juice (ab-e-gooreh); in my version, I've brought in sumac and fresh lemon juice for that tart zing. I love how just by combining a few simple ingredients and chopping them really fine, you can create a mouthwatering dish that you'll want to eat by the bowlful!

MAKES 4 TO 6 SERVINGS

1 large English cucumber or 5 small cucumbers, finely chopped

3 medium tomatoes, finely chopped

½ medium red onion, finely chopped

⅓ cup finely chopped cilantro

⅓ cup fresh mint, finely chopped, or 1 teaspoon dried mint

2 tablespoons olive oil

Juice of ½ lemon

1 teaspoon salt

1 teaspoon sumac

1 teaspoon ground black pepper

In a large bowl, combine the cucumber, tomatoes, onion, cilantro, and mint.

Drizzle the olive oil and lemon juice over the mixture.

Sprinkle the salt, sumac, and pepper on top, then toss to combine everything.

Let the salad sit in the fridge for 20 to 30 minutes before serving to allow all the flavors to incorporate.

KACHUMBER
(Indian Side Salad)

This fresh, bright, and simple salad is a mainstay in Indian homes and restaurants. It's an excellent side dish to curries or daals and especially popular alongside biryani, pilau, and tandoori chicken, but it's also great tucked into sandwiches, burgers, and wraps.

Each ingredient is raw and fresh, bringing a distinct texture and satisfying crunch. The lemon juice cuts through the earthy flavors of the other ingredients and offers a refreshing tanginess that balances the freshness of the vegetables. Finally, the spices lend it a warmth (or heat depending on how bold you're feeling) that dances on your tongue without being overpowering. Seriously, there are certain dishes that I'd almost rather not eat if they're not served with kachumber!

MAKES 4 SERVINGS

1 large onion, diced
2 large tomatoes, diced
1 green chile, thinly sliced
1 teaspoon lemon juice
2 tablespoons finely chopped cilantro
½ teaspoon salt
½ teaspoon ground red chile

Place all the ingredients in a bowl and toss. Allow the salad to sit for a few minutes for the flavors to come together.

Store in an airtight container in the fridge for up to 2 days.

Quinoa Herb Salad, p. 109

Fresh Greek Pasta Salad, p. 125

QUINOA HERB SALAD

This salad is a staple in our house. It is filling and packed with healthy nutrients—including loads of protein from the quinoa and chickpeas—and has a light, refreshing flavor from the simple citrus dressing. It's great on its own but also goes with everything from chicken to fish. Once you have the basic recipe down, you can add just about any veggies and herbs.

I like to portion out my salad in smaller mason jars or plastic containers. This keeps it fresher longer and makes for a quick grab-and-go lunch for Zee and the kids for the rest of the week!

MAKES 6 SERVINGS

SALAD
1 cup dry quinoa
1 (15-ounce) can chickpeas, drained and rinsed
3 baby cucumbers or 1 large English cucumber, diced
1 pint cherry tomatoes, halved
½ red bell pepper, diced
½ yellow bell pepper, diced
2 carrots, diced
3–4 kale leaves, torn into small pieces
¼ red onion, diced
½ cup sliced fresh mint
½ cup chopped cilantro
½ cup sliced basil leaves

DRESSING
Zest of 1 lemon
Zest of 1 lime
Juice of 1 lemon
Juice of 1 lime
¼ cup olive oil
Salt and pepper to taste

Prepare the quinoa according to the package directions. (I like to cook my quinoa in chicken or veggie stock to add flavor.) Let cool to room temperature.

Whisk all the dressing ingredients in a bowl or mix in a small mason jar.

Place all the salad ingredients in a large bowl and mix well. Pour the dressing over the top and give it all a good stir.

Store any leftover salad in an airtight container in the fridge for up to 5 days.

QUINOA CHICKPEA TABBOULEH

When I was young, my family traveled to Syria and Lebanon. There I had tabbouleh, the herb and bulgur salad, for the first time and just couldn't get enough of its fresh flavors. When we came back, I started adding parsley and mint to my salads and playing around with making my own dressings. This version of tabbouleh has the same delicious herb punch, but I've swapped the traditional bulgur wheat for quinoa. I've also added chickpeas to up the protein and fiber content to make it an even more filling salad!

MAKES 6 TO 8 SERVINGS

1 cup dry quinoa
1 pint cherry tomatoes, halved
1 (15-ounce) can chickpeas, drained and rinsed
1 small cucumber, diced
3 green onions, thinly sliced
1½ cups chopped dill
1½ cups chopped mint
2 cups chopped parsley
6 tablespoons olive oil
Juice of 1½ lemons
1 teaspoon honey
1 garlic clove, minced
2 teaspoons ground cumin
1 teaspoon paprika
1 teaspoon salt
1 teaspoon ground black pepper

Cook your quinoa according to the package directions. Transfer to a large bowl and let cool to room temperature.

To the bowl, add the tomatoes, chickpeas, cucumber, onions, dill, mint, and parsley. Toss to combine.

In a small bowl, whisk the olive oil, lemon juice, honey, garlic, cumin, paprika, salt, and pepper. Pour the dressing over your salad. Mix well and allow a few minutes for all the dressing flavors to absorb before serving.

Keep in an airtight container in the fridge for up to 3 days.

Quinoa Chickpea
Tabbouleh, p. 110

Red Cabbage
and Apple Slaw, p. 118

SPICED CHICKPEA AND CAULIFLOWER SALAD WITH LEMONY TAHINI DRESSING

This salad, with its mix of creamy, tender, and crunchy textures, is great on its own or as a side dish, and it can be served warm or cold. If you've never tried tahini, you're in for a treat. The delicious nutty flavor it adds to the dressing brings everything together. The dressing can be made ahead of time and stored in the fridge until you're ready to use it.

MAKES 6 SERVINGS

SALAD
1 head cauliflower, chopped into small florets
½ red onion, sliced
3 tablespoons olive oil
Salt and pepper to taste
1 (15-ounce) can chickpeas, drained and rinsed
½ teaspoon smoked paprika
¼ teaspoon garlic powder
⅛ teaspoon cayenne
½ bunch parsley, chopped

LEMONY TAHINI DRESSING
⅓ cup tahini
⅓ cup water
¼ cup lemon juice
2 garlic cloves, minced
½ teaspoon ground cumin
½ teaspoon cayenne
¼ teaspoon salt

Preheat the oven to 375°F.

Spread the cauliflower florets and the onion onto a large baking sheet. Drizzle the vegetables with 2 tablespoons of the olive oil and season with a pinch or two of salt and pepper to taste. Toss it all together before spreading out evenly. Roast for 20 minutes, stirring at the halfway mark, until the cauliflower is fork-tender. Remove the sheet from the oven and allow to cool slightly.

Pour the chickpeas onto another baking sheet. Drizzle with the remaining 1 tablespoon olive oil, sprinkle with the spices, and stir until the chickpeas are coated. Roast for 20 minutes, then turn on the broiler and broil for 1 to 2 minutes to make them extra crispy (watch carefully so they don't burn).

For the dressing, place the tahini, water, lemon juice, garlic, cumin, cayenne, and salt in a blender. Blend until smooth.

In a large bowl, combine the spiced chickpeas, cauliflower and onion, and parsley. Pour the dressing over the salad and toss to combine. Serve warm, or transfer to the refrigerator and let chill before serving cold.

This salad can be stored in an airtight container in the fridge for up to 3 days.

BRIGHT SUMMER KALE SALAD

This salad will make anybody love kale! Its secret weapons are sweet pops of pomegranate and summery strawberries. It's great to bring to a summer barbecue or a family gathering; even my kids enjoy it, and I promise, yours can too (bonus: massaging the kale is a fun way to get your kids involved in the kitchen). If you're making it ahead of time, wait to add the dressing and pumpkin seeds until just before serving.

MAKES 6 SERVINGS

1 large bunch kale, stems removed
1 teaspoon olive oil
Pinch of salt
1 large red apple, cored and diced
8 large strawberries, sliced
1 large English cucumber, chopped
Seeds from 1 large pomegranate
1 avocado, diced (optional)
¾ cup chopped cilantro
⅔ cup pumpkin seeds
2 tablespoons hemp hearts (optional)

DRESSING

¾ cup olive oil
½ cup fresh lemon juice
1 tablespoon honey
½ teaspoon minced ginger
½ teaspoon minced garlic
Salt and pepper to taste

Rip the kale leaves into large pieces and place in a large bowl. Pour the olive oil and a pinch of salt over the kale and massage the leaves with your hands until they soften. This helps break down the tough fibers.

Add the apple, strawberries, cucumber, pomegranate seeds, avocado (if using), and cilantro to the kale and toss to combine.

In a separate small bowl or mason jar, add all the dressing ingredients, mix well.

Dress the salad and add the pumpkin seeds and hemp hearts, if desired, a few minutes before serving.

NASIM'S GREEN MANGO AND APPLE SALAD

My mother-in-law, Nasim, is known for this salad. Whenever she serves it, everyone asks for the recipe. It's made with green mango—mango that hasn't ripened yet—which adds some crunch and tang to this great mix of fruits and veggies. (I use a mandoline to slice my fruit and vegetables, but if you don't have one, just Zen out and chop away!) The little spicy kick in the dressing will have you coming back for more. This salad is a perfect accompaniment for your next Thai food night and also goes beautifully with any stir-fry dish.

MAKES 6 SERVINGS

DRESSING

1 garlic clove, minced
1–2 teaspoons red pepper flakes
2 teaspoons brown sugar
1 teaspoon salt
Juice of 1 lime
2 teaspoons olive oil
1 teaspoon rice vinegar

SALAD

3 green mangoes, peeled and cut into long strips
2 red bell peppers, seeded and cut into long strips
1 green apple, thinly sliced
1 red onion, thinly sliced
½ cup chopped cilantro
¼ cup chopped mint
¼ cup peanuts or cashews, roughly chopped (optional)

Combine the dressing ingredients in a jar or a small bowl. Let the dressing rest for 10 minutes to let the flavors meld.

Toss the mangoes, peppers, apple, and onion in a large bowl, then add the dressing and toss again to coat everything well. Right before serving, sprinkle with the cilantro, mint, and peanuts, if desired.

RED CABBAGE AND APPLE SLAW WITH CITRUS DRESSING

If you're looking for a healthy alternative to typically creamy slaws, this fresh and zingy slaw will do just the trick. It's great as a side at a barbecue or even tossed into sandwiches and wraps.

MAKES 6 SERVINGS

CITRUS DRESSING

1 tablespoon fresh orange juice
1 tablespoon fresh lemon juice
3 tablespoons olive oil
1 tablespoon honey
1 tablespoon grainy mustard
1 tablespoon apple cider vinegar
Salt and pepper to taste

SLAW

1 bunch kale, stems removed, chopped into small strips
2 cups finely chopped red cabbage
2 red apples, chopped into matchsticks
1 large carrot, chopped into matchsticks
1 medium red onion, finely chopped
½ cup finely chopped fresh mint
⅓ cup dried cranberries

In a mason jar or small mixing bowl, combine all the dressing ingredients. Mix well and set aside.

In a large salad bowl, place the kale, red cabbage, apples, carrots, onion, and mint. About 15 minutes before serving, pour the dressing over the salad and toss well to make sure the dressing soaks into the kale and cabbage. Sprinkle the dried cranberries on top!

This salad can be stored in an airtight container in the fridge for up to 3 days.

BRUSSELS SPROUTS AND APPLE SALAD WITH MAPLE TAHINI DRESSING

Sometimes the least expected ingredients come together to make something wonderful. If you're looking to change it up from the typical salads, you have to give this one a try! The raw Brussels sprouts add a cabbagey flavor and, along with the apple and nuts, a satisfying crunch. But my favorite part is the dressing, great for any hearty salad.

MAKES 6 SERVINGS

1 pound Brussels sprouts, trimmed
1 large sweet apple, such as Honeycrisp, thinly sliced
¼ cup dried cranberries
¼ cup sliced almonds or walnuts, roughly chopped
¼ cup shaved Parmesan

DRESSING
½ cup tahini
½ cup warm filtered water
¼ cup lemon juice
1 tablespoon maple syrup
½ teaspoon sea salt
¼ teaspoon garlic powder
¼ teaspoon ground black pepper
Pinch of paprika

Using a food processor with a shredding disc or a mandoline, finely slice the Brussels sprouts and place into a salad bowl. Layer the apple slices on top. Top the salad with the cranberries and almonds.

To make the dressing, combine everything in a large bowl or mason jar and mix well. Add more water if needed to thin it out to a pourable consistency. Pour the dressing over the salad and toss a few minutes before serving to allow all the dressing to soak into the Brussels sprouts. When you're ready to serve, sprinkle with the shaved Parmesan.

LENTIL AND PARSLEY SALAD

Many people are looking for more vegetarian and meatless options to add to their roster, and with all the protein from the lentils and the savory feta, this salad is just as good a main as it is a side dish. (I like to use feta that has been marinated in spices for extra flavor.) If you like tabbouleh, you'll love this! This salad keeps really well in the fridge provided you keep the arugula and spinach separate, so I'll often make a big batch to have all week long and then toss in those greens right before we eat. And I always make extra to send over to my parents because my dad loves this salad so much!

MAKES 6 SERVINGS

SALAD

1 cup arugula
1 cup chopped baby spinach
½ cup chopped parsley
1 small red onion, diced
2 medium tomatoes, diced
1 English cucumber, diced
1 (15-ounce) can green
   lentils, drained and rinsed
½ cup cubed or crumbled
   feta

DRESSING

¼ cup olive oil
Juice of ½ lemon
1–2 garlic cloves, minced
1 teaspoon salt
1 teaspoon ground black
   pepper
1 teaspoon sumac

In a large bowl, toss together all the salad ingredients.

In a small bowl or mason jar, place all your dressing ingredients and mix or shake to combine well.

Pour the dressing over the salad and give it a toss.

NOTE: If you are making this salad in advance, hold the arugula and spinach when you combine the other ingredients. Add the leafy greens just before serving. This salad will keep in an airtight container in the fridge for up to 2 days.

THAI SALAD

It's all about the crunch with this Thai-inspired slaw. And yes, I'm asking you to grab one of those 99-cent instant ramen packages, discard the seasoning sachet, and crumble those crunchy noodles up. Trust me, you're going to love this salad! It's super simple to make, and the toasted almonds and seeds give it such a nice crunch paired with the fresh cabbage and green onions!

MAKES 6 SERVINGS

SALAD
1 tablespoon sesame oil
¼ cup sesame seeds
¼ cup sliced almonds
1 small head of cabbage,
    thinly sliced
4 green onions, thinly sliced
1 cup chopped cilantro
1 (3-ounce) packet ramen
    noodles, crumbled

DRESSING
¼ cup olive oil
2 tablespoons rice vinegar
1 tablespoon maple syrup
1 tablespoon soy sauce
1 large garlic clove, minced

Heat the sesame oil in a frying pan over medium heat. Add the sesame seeds and almonds and toast until just golden, for 1 to 2 minutes. Shake them onto a paper towel to absorb excess oil and allow them to cool.

In a large bowl, toss together the cabbage, green onions, cilantro, and crumbled ramen noodles.

In a small bowl or jar, add all the dressing ingredients and mix well.

Pour the dressing over your salad and toss. Top with the toasted seeds and nuts.

This salad will keep in the fridge for 1 day.

SOBA NOODLE AND TOFU SALAD WITH SESAME GINGER DRESSING

Have you ever had a "Hey, I can make this!" moment at a grocery store or restaurant? I had a soba noodle salad at Whole Foods one day, and it was so delish that I absolutely had to try re-creating it at home. I have to say mine turned out even better (and making it at home is more cost-effective, to boot!). I love how the noodles soak up the tangy dressing! This is a flexible recipe, so feel free to customize it depending on what you have on hand.

MAKES 4 SERVINGS

SOBA NOODLE AND TOFU SALAD

- 1 (8-ounce) package of soba noodles
- 2 teaspoons soy sauce
- 2 teaspoons sesame oil
- 1 cup firm tofu, cubed
- ¾ cup sliced mushrooms
- ¾ cup chopped asparagus (cut into 1-inch long pieces)
- 1 cup shredded carrot
- 1 cup shredded red cabbage
- ½ cup thinly sliced yellow bell pepper
- ½ cup chopped cilantro
- ¼ cup sesame seeds

SESAME GINGER DRESSING

- 3 tablespoons sesame oil
- 3 tablespoons soy sauce or coconut aminos
- 1 teaspoon coconut sugar
- 1 garlic clove, minced
- 1 large piece of ginger, grated
- 1 tablespoon Sriracha sauce (optional)
- Juice of ½ lime (optional)

Prepare the soba noodles according to the package directions. Drain and let the noodles cool to room temperature. Transfer to a large bowl and set aside.

While the soba noodles are cooking, whisk 1 teaspoon of the soy sauce and 1 teaspoon of the sesame oil in a medium bowl. And the cubed tofu and gently toss. Marinate for a few minutes.

Heat a frying pan over medium heat. Toss in the tofu and cook, turning occasionally, until the cubes are toasty brown on all sides, for 1 to 2 minutes per side. Remove from the pan and set aside.

In that same bowl, whisk the remaining 1 teaspoon soy sauce and 1 teaspoon sesame oil. Toss in your mushrooms and asparagus.

Sauté the vegetables in your pan until they are crisp-tender, for 5 to 7 minutes.

To the bowl with the soba noodles, add the tofu, asparagus and mushrooms, and the remaining salad ingredients and toss until well combined.

In a small bowl or jar, whisk or shake the dressing ingredients. Pour the dressing over the salad and toss again before serving.

This salad will keep in the fridge for about 2 days.

FRESH GREEK PASTA SALAD

Don't just relegate pasta salads to potluck dinners (although they're also great for those!). This one is Greek inspired, with briny olives, feta, and a homemade herby dressing and is so delicious we have it at home all the time for lunch or dinner. I love the combination of tender pasta with the crunchy veggies.

MAKES 6 SERVINGS

DRESSING

⅓ cup olive oil
2 tablespoons rice vinegar
1 teaspoon grainy mustard
1 garlic clove, minced
1½ teaspoons salt
1 teaspoon ground black pepper
1 teaspoon dried oregano
1 teaspoon dried basil
1 teaspoon lemon pepper

SALAD

1 (8-ounce) package of penne pasta, cooked according to package instructions
2 cups arugula
1 cup baby spinach
1 cup halved cherry tomatoes
¾ cup chopped cucumber
½ cup chopped red peppers
⅓ cup diced red onion
¼ cup chopped black olives
⅓ cup crumbled feta
¼ cup chopped parsley

In a small bowl or jar, place all the dressing ingredients and combine well. Set aside.

In a large bowl, toss all the salad ingredients together. Add the dressing and toss again to coat the pasta and vegetables.

This salad can be kept in the fridge for 1 to 2 days.

GRILLED CORN AND ZUCCHINI SALAD

You could make this salad anytime, but it's particularly great at the height of summer when zucchini and corn are in season. Where our family lives, in Ontario, Canada, the corn is so good we just want to find as many ways to enjoy it as possible!

**MAKES 4 TO 5
SERVINGS**

2–3 tablespoons olive oil
3 medium zucchini, thickly
　　sliced
2 cups corn kernels (fresh,
　　canned, or thawed from
　　frozen)
1 cup crumbled feta cheese
2 cups arugula
Juice of ½ lemon
Salt and pepper to taste

Heat a grill pan or frying pan over medium-high heat.

Drizzle 1½ tablespoons of the olive oil over the zucchini. Place the zucchini on the hot pan and cook until they begin to brown and char on the bottom, for 4 to 5 minutes, then flip and repeat on the other side. Remove the zucchini from the pan and set aside.

Add the corn to the hot pan and cook until golden brown, for 3 to 4 minutes.

Place the zucchini, corn, feta, and arugula in a large bowl and toss together. Drizzle the remaining olive oil (about 1 tablespoon) and the lemon juice over the salad. Season to taste with salt and pepper.

This salad will keep in the fridge for 1 or 2 days.

MANGO, FETA, AND GREENS

Mango, mint, and feta, oh my! In my opinion, this is the perfect summer salad. It's delicious—obviously—but it also looks so darn pretty. It's great alongside grilled chicken or fish but also delicious as a light lunch on its own. Mangoes in salads are just the best addition!

MAKES 6 SERVINGS

DRESSING

¼ cup olive oil
1 tablespoon lemon juice
1 tablespoon balsamic
   vinegar
1 tablespoon honey
1 teaspoon mustard
1 clove of garlic, minced
Salt and pepper to taste

SALAD

4 cups finely chopped
   lettuce
½ medium red onion,
   chopped
½ red pepper, chopped
1 large cucumber, chopped
1 large mango, peeled and
   chopped
1 tablespoon chopped fresh
   mint
1 tablespoon chopped fresh
   basil
⅓ cup crumbled feta

In a small bowl or jar, combine all the dressing ingredients and mix well.

In a large salad bowl, place the lettuce, onion, red pepper, cucumber, and mango. Top with the fresh herbs.

When you're ready to serve, add the dressing to the salad and top with the feta, and mix well.

This salad will keep in the fridge for 1 or 2 days.

FENNEL CITRUS SALAD WITH GREENS

Adding citrus to salad just takes things to another level. I love changing up the fruit I add to my salads, and the combination of fennel and oranges is so unique and adds an extra layer to this fresh, crisp salad! The dressing, made with the juice of the citrus, ties everything together well. This salad is as enjoyable to look at as it is to eat, and it will definitely impress whoever you're making it for! Use one regular orange and one blood orange for extra-vibrant color.

MAKES 4 SERVINGS

1 bunch kale (stems removed), chopped

1 small fennel bulb, thinly sliced

⅓ cup roughly chopped cilantro or mint, or a combination

½ English cucumber, sliced into half-moons

Seeds from ½ pomegranate

2 oranges, segmented, juices reserved

2 tablespoons roughly chopped pistachios

1 tablespoon goat cheese (optional)

DRESSING

3 tablespoons freshly squeezed orange juice

2 teaspoons Dijon mustard

2 tablespoons apple cider vinegar

2 tablespoons honey

¼ cup olive oil

1 teaspoon salt

½ teaspoon ground black pepper

In a large bowl, combine the kale, fennel, and cilantro. Mix until incorporated. Top with the cucumbers, pomegranate seeds, orange segments, pistachios, and goat cheese.

Combine the dressing ingredients in a jar with a lid. Close the jar and shake well till the dressing is emulsified.

Dress and toss the salad 5 minutes before serving.

This salad will keep in the fridge for 3 days.

DINNER

NOTHING MAKES ME HAPPIER THAN DINNER with family and friends. When it's just the four of us, the evening meal is a chance to hear about everybody's day, talk through work or school challenges, and just be together when no one has to rush off. And when we have friends or extended family over, it's a chance to hang out in the most relaxed way. I love people wandering into the kitchen to chat with me while I'm cooking; I love that we can linger at the table for hours if we feel like it. And of course, I love the food.

MY GO-TO DAL CURRY

Do you do Meatless Mondays? As much as we love our meat and chicken in my house, we try to have a few vegetarian meals a week. My favorite veggie meals are Indian curries. This combination of lentils and vegetables is super healthy, and thanks to the spices you get rich, bold flavors. I always have red lentils in the pantry because they cook really fast. This dal—a kind of curry—is a staple in our house. We love to have it with rice, roti, or bread with Kachumber (Indian Side Salad) (page 106) on the side.

MAKES 6 SERVINGS

1¼ cups red lentils
1 tablespoon neutral oil, such as canola or avocado
1 medium onion, chopped
1 teaspoon cumin seeds
1 tablespoon garlic paste (page 13)
1½ teaspoons ginger paste (page 13)
1 small green chile, chopped
1 teaspoon ground turmeric
1½ teaspoons ground cumin
1 teaspoon ground red chile
1½ teaspoons salt
1 medium tomato, chopped
1 cup frozen spinach, thawed
1 cup strained tomatoes
2 tablespoons coconut milk
1 tablespoon lemon juice
¼ cup chopped cilantro

Pour the lentils into a bowl and cover them with cold water. Soak for 15 to 30 minutes.

In a large pot, heat the oil over medium heat. Add the onion and cumin seeds and fry until fragrant and the onion becomes translucent, for 2 to 3 minutes. Add the garlic and ginger pastes and fry for a minute or so, then add the green chile and spices and cook until the spices are toasted and the pan becomes a little dry. Add the chopped tomato and cook until it begins to break down (you can add 1 or 2 tablespoons of water if it seems too dry), for 2 to 3 minutes. Add the spinach, strained tomatoes, and 1 cup of water. Mix well and cook until the sauce has thickened, 10 to 15 minutes.

Drain the lentils, add them to the pot, and simmer. Cover the pot with a lid and cook until the lentils are soft, for 8 to 10 minutes. Add another cup of water (or a little more or less, depending on how thick you would like the curry). Stir in the coconut milk and lemon juice. Sprinkle the top with cilantro and serve.

ALOO GOBI
(Indian Potato and Cauliflower Curry)

Cauliflower is such a great vegetable. It's inexpensive, super hearty, and it takes on the flavor of any spices it's cooked with. It took me a while to find the right recipe to get my kids on board with cauliflower, but when I found this one (where it's combined with delicious, soft potatoes and a tomato sauce made with Indian spices), they gobbled it right up! Serve the curry with rice, roti, or naan.

MAKES 4 TO 6 SERVINGS

3 medium tomatoes, chopped
2 tablespoons vegetable oil
1 teaspoon cumin seeds
2 bay leaves
1 medium onion, chopped
1 tablespoon garlic paste (page 13)
1 teaspoon salt
1 tablespoon ground turmeric
1 tablespoon garam masala
1 tablespoon ground red chile
1 teaspoon ground coriander
1 teaspoon ground cumin
2 fenugreek leaves (mehthi)
1 tablespoon tomato paste
1 medium head of cauliflower, chopped into 2-inch florets
3 medium potatoes, peeled and cubed
¼ cup chopped cilantro

In a blender, purée the tomatoes until smooth. Set aside.

Heat the oil in a large saucepan over medium-high heat. Add the cumin seeds and bay leaves and toast them until they're fragrant, about 1 minute. Add the onion and cook till it begins to brown and soften, for 2 to 3 minutes. Add the garlic paste and stir well to combine, then add the dry spices and toast until fragrant. Add the tomatoes and stir well. Let the mixture simmer for 4 to 5 minutes.

Add the fenugreek leaves and tomato paste and give it a stir.

Add the cauliflower and potatoes and mix well. Pour in ½ cup of water, stir, and then cover the pot. Simmer for 10 to 12 minutes until the cauliflower and potatoes are fork-tender.

Stir, then sprinkle cilantro on top and serve.

PALAK TOFU
(Spinach Tofu Curry)

You might have heard of palak paneer, the curry dish of spinach cooked along soft, mild Indian cheese. This recipe swaps the paneer for tofu with a few other twists that make that dairy-heavy Indian staple dish completely vegan.

I admit I used to be very nervous about cooking tofu at home and only ever had it at restaurants. But once I tried cooking with it, I realized how versatile tofu could be, and it gave me another great way to have a few plant-based meals up my sleeves. The moral of this tofu story is: don't be afraid to try making something new. It might end up being your signature dish!

MAKES 4 SERVINGS

3 tablespoons vegetable oil
1 (16-ounce) package of firm tofu, pressed and cut into ¾-inch cubes (see Tip)
1 medium onion, peeled and cut into quarters
1 large tomato, stem removed and halved
3 garlic cloves, peeled
1 (1½-inch) piece of ginger, peeled
1 small green chile, stem removed
Leaves from 1 small bunch cilantro (reserve some for garnish)
2 teaspoons cumin seeds
1 teaspoon fenugreek leaves (mehthi)
1 teaspoon ground red chile
1 teaspoon ground coriander
1 teaspoon ground cumin
1 teaspoon garam masala
½ teaspoon ground turmeric
1 teaspoon salt
1 (10-ounce) package of frozen spinach, thawed
⅓ cup coconut milk
2 tablespoons fresh lemon juice

In a large frying pan, heat 1 tablespoon of the oil over medium-high heat. Fry the tofu in batches, for 1 to 2 minutes on each side, allowing for space between the pieces so they crisp up. Transfer the cooked tofu to a plate as you work.

In a food processor or blender, combine the onion, tomato, garlic, ginger, green chile, and cilantro and blend into a smooth, thick sauce, scraping down the sides as needed.

In the same pan used for the tofu, heat the remaining oil over medium heat. Add the cumin seeds and fenugreek leaves and fry for a minute until fragrant. Add the dry spices and salt and toast them for a few minutes. Pour in the tomato sauce and cook for 3 to 4 minutes on medium-low until the sauce begins to bubble and the oil begins to separate. Toss in the spinach and mix well, allowing the spinach to heat up. Add the coconut milk and lemon and stir. Add the cooked tofu and mix gently. Top with the cilantro and serve with naan.

TIP: Pressing tofu helps to remove excess water, making it firmer in texture. You can press tofu with a tofu press or easily DIY with supplies you probably have in your kitchen. Drain the tofu well when you remove it from the package, then set it on a plate lined with a clean tea towel or paper towels. Place another towel over the top, then another plate, and weigh down the plate with something heavy (some heavy cookbooks or a heavy-bottomed pot, for instance). Press the tofu for about 30 minutes, then proceed with your recipe.

LAZY LASAGNA

This dish gives you all the flavor of a delicious, layered lasagna but comes together in half the time. Rather than a long bake in the oven, the dish is quickly broiled to finish it. Even better, it has tons of healthy veggies that you (and your kids!) might not even really notice in between all that meat sauce and cheese. I got in the habit of "hiding" veggies in this dish when my kids were younger and a bit pickier, and even though their palates are more adventurous now, I still pack in that veg and serve this with a big fresh salad to make it a very green meal indeed!

MAKES 6 TO 8 SERVINGS

1 (16-ounce) package of cut pasta, such as penne
1½ pounds ground beef (part regular, part lean)
1 large onion, chopped small
4 garlic cloves, minced
1 tablespoon minced ginger
2½ teaspoons dried oregano
2½ teaspoons paprika
2½ teaspoons red pepper flakes
3 teaspoons salt
1 large bell pepper, chopped small
1 large zucchini, chopped small
1 medium carrot, chopped small
1 (24-ounce) jar tomato sauce
2 cups baby spinach
1 tablespoon lemon zest
3 tablespoons butter
1 tablespoon flour
2½ cups milk
2 cups shredded mozzarella or Cheddar cheese
1 teaspoon salt
½ teaspoon ground black pepper
1 teaspoon lemon juice
½ cup bread crumbs
¼ cup chopped fresh parsley

Bring a large pot of water to a boil. Cook the pasta according to the package directions, then drain and set aside.

In a large frying pan, cook the ground beef over medium heat, breaking it up as it cooks, until it begins to brown and release liquid, about 5 minutes. Add the onions, garlic, ginger, spices, and salt and stir to incorporate. Cook for a few minutes until the onion begins to soften. Toss in the chopped veggies and continue to cook, stirring occasionally so the meat doesn't stick to the bottom of the pan, until the veggies begin to soften. Pour in the tomato sauce and add the spinach and lemon zest. Stir well and bring the sauce to a simmer. Cover and cook until the veggies are broken down, for 5 to 6 minutes. Add ½ cup of water if the sauce seems too thick.

Now, on to the cheese sauce! In the same pot you used for the pasta, melt the butter over medium heat. Whisk in the flour and cook, continuing to stir, until it foams and browns lightly. Slowly pour in the milk and cook, whisking all the while, until the sauce thickens enough that you can create a line at the bottom of the pot with a wooden spoon. Lower the heat to low. Add 1 cup of the cheese plus the salt and pepper and mix until the cheese is completely melted and incorporated. Stir in the lemon juice. Add the cooked pasta and stir to completely coat it in the sauce.

Heat the oven to broil. Spread the cheesy pasta in the bottom of a large casserole dish. Layer the meat sauce over the pasta and spread it out evenly. Top with the remaining cheese and the bread crumbs.

Broil until the cheese melts and the top browns slightly, for 2 to 3 minutes. Remove from the oven and sprinkle with the fresh parsley. Serve immediately.

HEARTY SWEET POTATO CHILI

The sweet potato in this chili makes this vegetarian dinner hearty enough to compete with your old standby beef chili recipe. It's a warm and filling dinner that leaves you feeling so good because it's packed with veggies, fiber, and of course, flavor. To really take it to the next level, set out toppings like shredded cheese, sour cream, diced avocado, and crushed tortilla chips and let everyone load up their bowls.

MAKES 8 SERVINGS

3 tablespoons neutral oil, such as avocado
1 medium onion, chopped
3 garlic cloves, minced
1 large carrot, diced
1 green bell pepper, diced
1 cup frozen corn kernels
1 large sweet potato, cubed
2 cups thinly sliced kale
1 jalapeño, minced
2–3 tablespoons taco seasoning
3 teaspoons ground cumin
2 teaspoons chili powder
2 teaspoons salt
1 (14-ounce) can black beans, drained
1 (14.5-ounce) can crushed tomatoes
1 (24-ounce) jar strained tomatoes
1 tablespoon tomato paste
¼ cup chopped cilantro

TOPPINGS
Shredded Cheddar cheese
Sour cream
Chopped cilantro
Diced avocado
Crushed tortilla chips

Heat the oil in a large pot over medium-high heat. Add the onion and garlic and stir until fragrant and golden, for 2 to 3 minutes. Toss in the carrot, bell pepper, corn, sweet potato, kale, and jalapeño and stir; cook for 5 to 8 minutes until the veggies begin to soften. Add the taco seasoning (start with 2 tablespoons), cumin, chili powder, and salt and stir to incorporate. Add the black beans and crushed tomatoes and cook for 3 to 5 minutes until the tomatoes begin to break down. Add the strained tomatoes and stir. Simmer for 10 to 15 minutes until the sauce begins to bubble. Add the tomato paste and cook for another 5 minutes.

Have a taste and see what you think. I often add more taco seasoning and salt—but you do you! Cover the chili and simmer for another 15 to 20 minutes to allow the flavors to come together and the chili to thicken. If it's getting too thick, thin it out with a little water.

Sprinkle it with the cilantro just before serving.

Ladle the chili into bowls. Serve the toppings in their own bowls so people can load up their chili with whatever they like.

QUICK WEEKNIGHT NOODLES WITH CRISPY TOFU AND GREENS

There's something about warm noodles that just hits the spot! These slurpable noodles with a spicy, peanut buttery sauce are so easy and quick to whip up. Green vegetables like bok choy or broccolini brighten up the flavor. The tofu adds a nice crispy texture and a hit of protein, but it's completely optional if you don't have any handy or prefer to omit it.

MAKES 4 TO 6 SERVINGS

NOODLES

¾ package of rice noodles
2 tablespoons sesame oil
1 (16-ounce) package of firm tofu, pressed (see Tip on page 139), cut in ¼-inch thick slices
1½ teaspoons soy sauce
½ teaspoon sesame seeds
4–5 bok choy, quartered, or 1 bunch broccolini or Chinese broccoli, cut lengthwise

SAUCE

2 garlic cloves, chopped
1 (1-inch) piece ginger, chopped
¼ cup chopped cilantro
3 green onions, chopped, plus more for garnish
1 teaspoon red pepper flakes
2 tablespoons soy sauce
1 tablespoon chile garlic sauce
1 tablespoon peanut butter
3 tablespoons neutral oil, such as avocado

Bring a large pot of water to a boil. Prepare the noodles according to the package instructions. Reserve ½ cup of the cooking water. Drain the noodles and set aside.

Heat 1 tablespoon of the sesame oil in a large nonstick skillet over medium heat. Add the tofu, soy sauce, and sesame seeds. Cook the tofu, turning occasionally, until it browns and crisps up on all sides, about 2 minutes per side. Remove the tofu from the pan and set aside.

In the same skillet, heat the remaining 1 tablespoon sesame oil over medium-high heat. Add the bok choy and cook until they begin to soften and get a nice char underneath (I like them a little crunchy), about 2 minutes.

To make the sauce: In a large heatproof bowl, combine the garlic, ginger, cilantro, green onion, red pepper flakes, soy sauce, chile garlic sauce, and peanut butter. Heat the avocado oil in a small pan until hot and pour it over the other sauce ingredients. Mix well to combine. Add the cooked noodles and toss to coat. Divide the noodles into bowls and top with tofu, bok choy, and more green onion. Serve hot.

EAST AFRICAN BIRYANI

Biryani, a mixed rice dish, is the ultimate party food! It's a staple on Eid (the celebration that marks the end of Ramadan fasting) and at any Indian or East African wedding you might attend. There are so many different variations of biryani, but this one is the one I grew up with. It's a thick tomato gravy with meat cooked till very soft, heaped onto fragrant basmati rice cooked with whole spices. As you can see from the ingredients list, this is an involved recipe, with many ingredients to build layers of flavor. To save some time, you can marinate the meat a day or two ahead and keep it in an airtight container in the fridge. Enjoy with Kachumber (Indian Side Salad) (page 106) and Gajar Athano (Pickled Carrots) (page 20).

MAKES 7 TO 8 SERVINGS

MARINADE

½ cup plain yogurt
1 teaspoon salt
1 tablespoon garlic paste (page 13)
1 tablespoon ginger paste (page 13)
1 tablespoon tomato paste
1 teaspoon ground red chile
1 teaspoon garam masala
1 tablespoon green chutney (page 14)
1 tablespoon chopped cilantro, plus more for garnish
Pinch of saffron
Juice of 1 lemon
1 tablespoon vegetable oil
4–5 black peppercorns
2 whole cloves
2 cardamom pods, crushed

MEAT AND POTATOES

2 pounds veal or lamb, cut into 1½-inch cubes
1 tablespoon vegetable oil
4 potatoes, peeled and quartered

First, marinate your meat; this can be done ahead of time. To make the marinade, combine all the marinade ingredients in a large bowl.

Add the meat to the bowl and stir to completely coat. Cover and refrigerate for at least 4 hours or up to 2 days. Bring the meat to room temperature before cooking.

Next, parcook the potatoes. You can either pan-fry or air-fry them. To pan-fry, heat the vegetable oil in a large frying pan over medium-high heat. Add the potatoes and pan-fry for 2 to 3 minutes per side until they are almost completely cooked through. They will finish cooking in the Biryani Gravy. To air-fry, spray or coat the potatoes with cooking oil and fry at 400°F for 15 minutes. Flip or shake the basket halfway through cooking time to make sure the potatoes are cooked evenly on all sides. Transfer the potatoes to a paper towel–lined plate to absorb excess oil.

While the potatoes are cooking, rinse the rice under cold water in a mesh strainer. Transfer the rice to a bowl and cover with cold water to soak while you continue with the recipe.

Next, you'll make the Biryani Gravy. Heat the oil in a large pot over medium heat. Add the tomatoes and cook until they start to break down and the oil separates, for 3 to 4 minutes. Add the garlic and ginger pastes, green chiles, cinnamon stick, and salt and mix well, cooking for another 3 to 4 minutes. Add the marinated meat and stir to combine. Bring the mixture to a simmer and cook for about 30 minutes until the gravy has thickened. Add the yogurt, tomato paste, fried onions, and 3 cups

(Continued)

RICE

2½ cups basmati rice
2 tablespoons vegetable oil
2 cinnamon sticks
3 cardamom pods, crushed
3 whole cloves
2 teaspoons salt
½ teaspoon saffron
⅓ cup warm milk
⅓ cup fried crispy onions
    (see Kitchen Staples,
    page 7)

BIRYANI GRAVY

3 tablespoons vegetable oil
3 tomatoes, finely chopped
1 teaspoon garlic paste
    (page 13)
1 teaspoon ginger paste
    (page 13)
2 green chiles, chopped
1 cinnamon stick
1½ teaspoons salt
¼ cup fresh plain yogurt, at
    room temperature
1 tablespoon tomato paste
1 cup fried crispy onions (see
    Kitchen Staples, page 7),
    plus more for garnish

of water and mix well. Lower the heat to low, cover your pot, and simmer for 30 to 35 minutes, until the meat is tender. Add the fried potatoes and mix well to combine everything.

While the meat and gravy are cooking, prepare the rice. Drain the soaked rice in a mesh strainer. Bring a large pot of water to a boil. Place 1 tablespoon of the oil plus the cinnamon, cardamom, cloves, and salt in the water. Add the drained rice and boil for 10 minutes, or until the rice is almost done. Drain the parcooked rice in a strainer. Stir together the saffron and warm milk in a glass measuring cup. Return the drained rice to the same pot. Top with the remaining 1 tablespoon of oil, the saffron milk, and the fried onions. Cover with a tight-fitting lid and simmer on low for another 15 minutes or until the rice is cooked and fluffy.

Spoon the fragrant rice onto a large platter, then top with the meat and gravy. Sprinkle with a little more cilantro and fried onions.

MASALA FISH WITH INDIAN POTATOES

When I was growing up, every Wednesday was fish night in our household. My dad would say that fish on Wednesday would bless your house with wealth, slyly adding, "Wealth isn't just money, you know."

Fish and potatoes are a universal combination. I guess you can call this my version of fish and chips, with more spices and pan-fried rather than breaded and deep-fried. I like to use halibut or haddock for this recipe—flaky white fish cooks quickly and takes up the spicy marinade really well.

MAKES 4 SERVINGS

FISH AND MARINADE

4 large white fish fillets
2 tablespoons canola oil
2 tablespoons lemon juice
1 tablespoon crushed or puréed tomatoes (see Tip)
1 teaspoon ginger paste (page 13)
1 teaspoon garlic paste (page 13)
1 teaspoon ground coriander
1 teaspoon ground cumin
1 teaspoon ground red chile
½ teaspoon ground turmeric
½ teaspoon salt

POTATOES AND SEASONING

3–4 medium potatoes, sliced into ¼-inch-thick rounds
1 tablespoon tomato paste
1 teaspoon ground red chile
1 teaspoon ground turmeric
1 teaspoon salt
2 tablespoons neutral oil
½ teaspoon crushed dried curry leaves

GARNISH

2 tablespoons chopped cilantro
1 small lemon, cut into wedges

Pat the fish dry with paper towels.

In a large, shallow bowl, place all the marinade ingredients and mix well. Add the fish and carefully turn each piece over a couple of times so they're completely coated with marinade. Marinate for 15 to 20 minutes at room temperature.

Bring a medium pot of salted water to a boil. Put in the potatoes and boil for 4 to 5 minutes until they are just beginning to cook but still very firm. Drain and set aside.

In a small bowl, mix the potato seasoning: tomato paste, ground red chile, turmeric, and salt. Set aside.

Heat 1 tablespoon of the oil in a large frying pan over medium heat. Add the fish and cook until it is opaque and flakes easily with a fork, for 4 to 5 minutes per side. Remove the fish to a serving plate.

Pour the remaining tablespoon of oil into the same pan and increase the heat to medium-high. Add the curry leaves and cook for 30 seconds, until fragrant. Add the potato seasoning and cook for 2 to 3 minutes. Toss in the cooked potatoes and gently stir to coat with the mixture. Simmer until the potatoes are cooked through, about another 5 minutes.

Spoon the potatoes onto the platter next to the fish. Sprinkle with cilantro and scatter lemon wedges around the dish. Serve hot.

TIP: Recipes often call for a small amount of particular ingredients (tomato paste, tomato purée, or crushed tomatoes). Then, of course, you are left with extra! My solution? I keep the excess fresh by spooning it into an ice cube tray, then storing the frozen cubes in baggies in the freezer. Next time you'll have the perfect portion on hand.

MASALA SHRIMP WRAPS

Shrimp is my go-to protein for busy days, and I always have some in the freezer. I love that I can defrost and cook them—all in 30 minutes. My kids and I love shrimp. Zee, not so much, but even he enjoys shrimp when I serve them up this way: flavored with warming spices and wrapped up in roti as delicious little packages of flavor. And these wraps are so quick to make. You just toss your shrimp in the spices, pan-fry them, make a quick raita, and fill up your roti!

MAKES 5 WRAPS

20–24 tiger shrimp, peeled, tails removed, and deveined
2 tablespoons chopped cilantro
1 teaspoon cumin seeds
1 teaspoon salt
½ teaspoon ground red chile
½ teaspoon ground turmeric
½ teaspoon ground cumin
½ teaspoon ground coriander
2 tablespoons neutral oil
Juice of ½ lemon
½ cup plain yogurt
1 tablespoon green chutney (page 14)
6 roti (page 192) or paratha
Chopped tomatoes, for topping
Thinly sliced red onion, for topping
Lemon wedges, for garnish

Rinse and pat dry the shrimp with paper towels and set aside.

In a large bowl, mix the cilantro, cumin seeds, salt, ground red chile, turmeric, cumin, coriander, 1 tablespoon of the oil, and lemon juice. Add the shrimp and give them a good toss. Marinate for 15 to 20 minutes at room temperature.

Heat the remaining tablespoon of oil in a frying pan over medium-high heat. Add the shrimp, keeping space between each piece so they will crisp nicely. Cook for 3 minutes, then flip the shrimp over and cook for another 2 minutes until they are pink all over.

In a small bowl, stir together the yogurt and green chutney to make a quick raita.

To make each wrap, place a roti on a plate. Spread it with raita and top with tomato, onion, shrimp, and a squeeze of lemon juice.

MUTHIYA
(Veggie Stew with Dumplings)

Comfort food at its finest, this is a super hearty stew packed with meat, lentils, a ton of vegetables, and spiced millet dumplings called muthiya, from which the dish takes its name. It can feed a village and only gets better the next day. Only people from our specific culture, South Asians from East Africa, seem to make muthiya, so I wanted to preserve and share the recipe in this book. The trouble was, I didn't know how to make it, and my mom, like many home cooks, never wrote down her exact recipe before, relying on memory and her cooking instincts to make it. We eventually got the specifics translated onto paper and I am so thrilled that I can make muthiya myself—and now so can you!

MAKES 14 TO 16 SERVINGS

DUMPLINGS
- 1½ cups millet flour
- 1 cup cooked small red beans
- 3 teaspoons salt
- 2 teaspoons ground red chile
- 2 teaspoons ground turmeric
- 1 teaspoon garlic paste (page 13)
- ½ teaspoon ground coriander
- ½ teaspoon ground cumin
- 2 tablespoons vegetable oil
- 2 (13-ounce) cans coconut milk

MEAT
- 2 pounds stew meat, cut into chunks
- 1 tablespoon garlic paste (page 13)
- 1 tablespoon ginger paste (page 13)
- 1 teaspoon salt

Make the dumplings first. Combine the millet flour, beans, 2 teaspoons of the salt, 1 teaspoon of the ground red chile, 1 teaspoon of the turmeric, the garlic paste, coriander, cumin, and vegetable oil in a mixing bowl. Stir until well incorporated. Add ½ cup water and mix until you create a dough. Scoop a tablespoonful of the dough and shape it with your hands to create an oval shape and set aside on a plate. Repeat until you have used up all your dough; you'll have about twelve to fifteen dumplings.

For the meat: Put the meat, garlic and ginger pastes, and salt into a pressure cooker or Instant Pot. Pour in 2 cups of water. Lock the lid into place and set to sealing. Cook on high pressure for 15 minutes. Release the pressure naturally for 10 minutes, then release the remaining pressure manually, press CANCEL, and remove the lid.

To make the stew, heat the oil in a very large pot over medium-high heat. Toss in the onions and fry until they begin to turn golden brown, for 3 to 4 minutes. Add the fenugreek leaves, fry for 1 minute, then add the spinach, chickpeas, mixed vegetables, cluster beans, pigeon peas, and potatoes; mix well to combine, and cook for 4 to 5 minutes. Add the rest of the ingredients for the stew except the lime, garam masala, and cilantro. Bring to a boil, then simmer for 30 minutes till the potatoes and eggplant are cooked to fork-tender. Add the cooked meat and give everything a stir.

(Continued)

1 tablespoon vegetable oil

3 medium onions, finely chopped

½ cup fenugreek leaves (mehthi)

1 (10-ounce) package of frozen spinach, thawed and the water squeezed out

1 cup split chickpeas (chana dal), soaked overnight and drained

3 cups frozen mixed vegetables, thawed

1 cup cluster beans (guvar; see Tip)

1 (15-ounce) can pigeon peas, drained

6 medium potatoes, peeled and cut into 1½-inch cubes

1 tablespoon garlic paste (page 13)

1 (14-ounce) can crushed tomatoes

3 tablespoons tomato paste

2 tablespoons salt

2 teaspoons ground red chile

1 teaspoon ground turmeric

2½ teaspoons ground coriander

2½ teaspoons ground cumin

2 long eggplants, cut lengthwise and then into half circles

4 cups water

Juice of 2 limes

1 tablespoon garam masala

¼ cup cilantro

In a large pot, heat the coconut milk and the remaining 1 teaspoon salt, 1 teaspoon ground red chile, and 1 teaspoon turmeric and bring to a simmer. Add the dumplings and simmer for 5 minutes, until the dumplings are cooked through.

Transfer the coconut mix and dumplings to the stew. Stir gently to combine everything, trying not to break the dumplings. Add the lime juice, garam masala, and cilantro. Cover and cook for another 20 minutes on low heat. Give everything a good stir, scraping the bottom of the pan to lift anything that has stuck to it. Taste for seasoning and adjust salt or ground red chile if needed.

Serve hot in bowls.

This stew will keep in the fridge for 5 days or freeze in well-sealed containers for up to 2 months.

TIP: Cluster beans, also known as guvar or guar, are small green beans that grow in pods. Most of the world's cluster beans are grown in India, and it's rare to find them fresh in North America, but they can be found in the freezer section of most South Asian grocery stores. If you cannot find them, you can substitute green beans or peas.

THAI-STYLE SHRIMP COCONUT CURRY

Coconut adds such a depth of flavor to any food, sweet or savory. In a curry, its creamy, mellow flavor elevates the spices and adds an unbeatable richness to the other ingredients. This weeknight favorite dish is flavored with bold, spicy red curry paste. Look for curry paste in the international food aisle of your grocery store. This might substitute your weekly Thai curry takeout. Yes! It's that good!

MAKES 6 SERVINGS

2 tablespoons coconut oil
1 medium onion, thinly
  chopped
3 garlic cloves, minced
2 teaspoons curry powder
1 teaspoon garam masala
1 teaspoon ground turmeric
1 teaspoon salt
½ red bell pepper, chopped
2 tablespoons Thai red
  curry paste
3 cups fresh spinach
20–24 tiger shrimp, peeled,
  deveined, and tails
  removed
1 (13-ounce) can coconut
  milk
Cooked basmati or jasmine
  rice, for serving
¼ cup chopped cilantro
Juice of 1 lime

Heat the oil in a large, deep-frying pan over medium-high heat. Add the onion and cook, stirring, until it begins to soften, for 2 to 3 minutes. Add the garlic and cook until fragrant, for 1 minute more. Add the curry powder, garam masala, turmeric, and salt and toast for a minute or two. Add the red pepper and mix well. (If the spices are becoming too dry, add 2 tablespoons of water and use a spoon to gently scrape the spices from the bottom of the pan.) Add the red curry paste and stir to coat the vegetables, then add the spinach and cook until it wilts. Toss in the shrimp, stir well, and cook until they start to turn pink, for 3 to 4 minutes. Pour in the coconut milk and stir to combine. Simmer the curry for 2 to 3 minutes.

When you're ready to serve, spoon the curry over the rice and top with the cilantro and lime juice.

LEMONY SHRIMP MARINARA PASTA

This is a great recipe to have in your back pocket for a quick weeknight dinner that will please the whole family (what kid doesn't love pasta?). It's simple, delicious, and brightened with lemon zest and a little kick of spice. Serve it with a fresh salad, such as Quinoa Herb Salad on page 109. I bet you'll have it in your regular rotation in no time.

MAKES 4 SERVINGS

1 (1-pound) package of spaghetti or penne pasta
2 tablespoons olive oil
3 garlic cloves, minced
1 tablespoon plus 1 teaspoon red pepper flakes (optional)
1 teaspoon salt
1 teaspoon ground black pepper
1 tablespoon fresh lemon juice
2 teaspoons lemon zest
20–24 raw shrimp, peeled, tails removed, and deveined
1 medium onion, chopped
2 cups chopped spinach
1 teaspoon dried oregano
1 (24-ounce) jar of your favorite marinara sauce
4–5 fresh basil leaves, chopped
Grated Parmesan cheese, for garnish

Bring a large pot of salted water to a boil and cook the pasta according to the package directions. Drain, reserving 1 cup of the pasta water, and set aside.

In a medium-sized bowl, combine 1 tablespoon of the olive oil, garlic, 1 tablespoon of the red pepper flakes (if using), salt, pepper, lemon juice, and lemon zest. Add the shrimp and stir gently to coat in the marinade. Marinate for 15 to 20 minutes at room temperature.

In a large frying pan, heat the remaining olive oil on medium heat. Add the onion and cook until it starts to soften, for 2 to 3 minutes. Add the spinach and oregano and cook until the spinach begins to wilt, for 3 minutes. Add the shrimp and cook till the shrimp begins to turn pink, for 3 minutes more. Pour in the marinara sauce and 1 teaspoon of red pepper flakes if you like a bit of spice. Simmer the sauce on low.

Add the reserved pasta water and pasta. Mix everything until the pasta is well coated with sauce. Heat through, then top with the basil leaves and Parmesan.

BUTTER CHICKEN

It's everyone's favorite Indian curry! My mom never made butter chicken when I was growing up, so it wasn't part of my repertoire, but we would order it at Indian restaurants. When my little guy, Ahmed, started eating solid foods, butter chicken was his absolute favorite thing in the world. As he grew up, he would try it at any restaurant that served it. Some were amazing and some not so much. So I figured I might as well learn how to make it at home to keep up with the demand. Through a little trial and error, I ended up with this delicious recipe. The chicken is marinated in yogurt and spices and cooked to sear in the flavor. Then it's added to the delicious, spicy, creamy tomato sauce for a dish that just melts in your mouth! This curry is delicious served over basmati rice, with warm naan, inside Loaded Sweet Potatoes (page 65), or even as a pizza topping, as Ahmed now enjoys (page 73).

MAKES 6 TO 8 SERVINGS

CHICKEN AND MARINADE

½ cup plain yogurt
1½ tablespoons minced garlic
1 tablespoon minced ginger
2 teaspoons garam masala
1 teaspoon ground turmeric
1 teaspoon ground cumin
1 teaspoon ground red chile
1 teaspoon salt
2 pounds boneless, skinless chicken thighs or breasts, cut into bite-sized pieces

In a large bowl, combine the ingredients for the chicken marinade. Add the chicken and stir until it is coated completely. Cover the bowl and refrigerate for at least 30 minutes up to overnight.

When you're ready to cook, warm the oil in a large heavy-bottomed skillet over medium heat. Working in batches so as not to crowd the pan, cook the chicken until browned all over, for 5 to 6 minutes per side. Remove the cooked chicken to a plate and set aside.

In the same pan, place the ghee and scrape up any brown bits from the bottom of the pan. Add the onion and ginger and cook until lightly browned and fragrant, for 2 to 3 minutes. Add the dry spices and toast for 1 to 2 minutes. Add the tomatoes, ground red chile, and salt. Mix everything well and continue to cook, using the back of a spoon to break up the tomatoes, until the sauce starts to darken in color. Add ¼ cup of water and the sugar and mix into the sauce.

Remove the sauce from the heat and blend until smooth, either with an immersion blender in the pan or working in batches with a regular blender.

Return the sauce in the pan to medium heat. Add the cooked chicken and its juices and stir well. Add the cream and mix until combined.

Top with the fenugreek, cilantro, and a little extra cream for presentation.

SAUCE

2 tablespoons canola oil

2 tablespoons ghee or butter

1 large onion, sliced or chopped

1 tablespoon minced or finely grated ginger

1½ teaspoons ground cumin

1½ teaspoons garam masala

1 teaspoon ground coriander

1 (14-ounce) can crushed tomatoes or 3 medium tomatoes, finely chopped

1 teaspoon ground red chile or Kashmiri chile

1¼ teaspoons salt

½ teaspoon sugar

1 cup heavy cream or evaporated milk, plus more for garnish

½ teaspoon fenugreek leaves (mehthi)

2 tablespoons cilantro

CHICKEN FRIED RICE

A recipe where leftovers from other meals become a delicious dinner? That's what I call a perfect weeknight meal. If you have the basics of the recipe—leftover chicken, such as my Spicy Soy Chicken (from the wraps recipe on page 77), and some leftover rice—you can use this recipe flexibly depending on what vegetables you have on hand. You can even change it up by using brown rice or cauliflower rice. Best of all, it's a one-pan meal that will satisfy everyone in the family.

MAKES 4 SERVINGS
AS A MEAL,
6 SERVINGS AS A SIDE

2 tablespoons soy sauce
½ tablespoon dark soy
    sauce (or more soy sauce)
½ tablespoon sambal oelek
    (see Note) or Sriracha
½ tablespoon oyster sauce
1½ tablespoons sesame oil
1 large onion, diced
2 garlic cloves, minced
1 teaspoon ginger, minced
1 cup frozen mixed
    vegetables, thawed
½ cup frozen corn, thawed
2 cups cooked shredded
    chicken (page 77)
4 cups cooked jasmine,
    brown, or cauliflower rice
2 eggs, beaten
Sliced green onion, for
    garnish
Sesame seeds, for garnish

In a small bowl, stir together the soy sauce, dark soy sauce, sambal oelek, and oyster sauce and set aside.

In a large wok or frying pan, heat 1 tablespoon of the sesame oil over medium heat. Add the onion, garlic, and ginger and cook until the onion begins to soften, for 2 to 3 minutes. Add the veggies and mix well for 2 minutes. Then add the cooked chicken and stir. Toss in the cooked, cold rice and blend with the chicken and vegetables, cooking for 1 to 2 minutes. Pour the sauce over everything and combine. Cook until the rice darkens and absorbs the sauce.

Make a well in the center of your rice mixture, add the remaining ½ tablespoon sesame oil, and pour in the eggs. Cook the eggs while stirring until they begin to scramble. Once they are almost fully cooked, mix in with the rest of the ingredients and cook until the scrambled egg is incorporated.

Serve topped with green onion and sesame seeds.

NOTE: Sambal oelek is an Indonesian chili sauce; it is spicy like Sriracha but has a complex flavor all its own.

ONE-POT PASTA WITH CHICKEN AND SUN-DRIED TOMATOES

This simple pasta is so packed with flavor—rich, bright, and just a bit of heat—that I think it will become as popular in your home as it is in mine. It's *almost* a one-pot meal and that just makes it even better. The chicken and pasta are cooked in the oil drained from a jar of sun-dried tomatoes to infuse everything with extra flavor.

MAKES 4 SERVINGS

1 (16-ounce) package of penne
1 teaspoon oil from sun-dried tomatoes
1 tablespoon butter
1 medium onion, chopped
4 garlic cloves, minced
1½ pounds boneless, skinless chicken breasts, cut in 1-inch cubes
1 tablespoon plus 2 teaspoons red pepper flakes
1 tablespoon dried oregano
1 tablespoon paprika
Salt and pepper to taste
¼ cup cream or milk
3 tablespoons shredded Parmesan cheese
2 tablespoons chopped sun-dried tomatoes
1 tablespoon pesto
1 tablespoon cream cheese, softened
2 cups chopped spinach
1 teaspoon lemon zest
Fresh basil, chopped, for garnish

Cook the penne pasta according to the package directions. Drain and set aside.

In the same pot, heat the oil and butter on medium-high heat. Add the onion and garlic and cook for 2 minutes until they begin to brown.

Add the chicken and stir to coat in the onion mixture. Cook until the chicken is browned on the edges, then add 1 tablespoon of the red pepper flakes, the oregano, paprika, and salt and pepper and mix well. Allow the chicken to cook in the spices for another 3 to 4 minutes until cooked through.

Add the cream, Parmesan cheese, tomatoes, and pesto and stir well to create a creamy sauce. Add the cream cheese and allow it to melt into the sauce. Stir in the spinach and cook until it begins to wilt, for 2 minutes. Bring the sauce to a simmer, then add the cooked pasta and toss to combine. Remove the pot from the heat and stir in the lemon zest.

Serve with extra red pepper flakes on the side and top with the basil.

KUKU PAKA
(Coconut Chicken Curry with Potatoes)

Kuku Paka is an East African dish of browned chicken cooked in a turmeric–coconut cream sauce. These beautiful flavors remind me of where my parents grew up. I like to make this with bone-in chicken for the extra flavor, but you can use boneless chicken if you prefer. Serve it with basmati rice or roti.

MAKES 6 SERVINGS

CHICKEN AND MARINADE

1 tablespoon garlic paste
 (page 13)
1 tablespoon ginger paste
 (page 13)
1 teaspoon salt
1 teaspoon ground black
 pepper
1 tablespoon green chutney
 (page 14)
Juice of ½ lemon
1½ pounds skinless, bone-in
 chicken pieces

CURRY

1 small tomato, roughly
 chopped
1 small onion, peeled and
 roughly chopped
1 teaspoon ground turmeric
1 teaspoon salt
1 tablespoon flour or
 cornstarch
1 (13-ounce) can coconut milk
2 tablespoons fresh lemon
 juice, plus more as needed
1 tablespoon green chutney
 (page 14)
2 tablespoons neutral oil
3 medium potatoes, cut into
 1½-inch cubes
¾ teaspoon garam masala
Cilantro, for garnish

In a large bowl, mix the garlic and ginger pastes, salt, pepper, green chutney, and lemon juice for the marinade. Add the chicken pieces and stir until they're completely coated. Cover and place in the fridge for at least 30 minutes and up to a few hours.

Preheat the broiler and position an oven rack on the highest position. Spread out the marinated chicken on a rimmed baking sheet and broil until browned on top, for 5 minutes, then flip and brown on the other side, for 4 to 5 minutes more. Note: the chicken does not need to cook through now; it will finish in the sauce.

To make the curry: In a blender, purée the tomato, onion, turmeric, salt, flour, coconut milk, lemon juice, and green chutney into a smooth sauce.

In a large saucepan, heat the oil over medium-high heat. Add the potatoes and cook for 5 to 7 minutes until they begin to brown lightly on the outside. Pour the curry over the potatoes and bring to a simmer. Add the broiled chicken and the juices from the baking tray. Simmer for 20 to 25 minutes until the chicken is cooked through and the potatoes are fork-tender.

Add more lemon juice and salt to taste. Sprinkle with the garam masala and garnish with cilantro.

SHEET PAN SUMAC CHICKEN WITH CARROTS AND CAULIFLOWER

This is not your average sheet-pan dinner. With its delicious spices and gorgeous colors, it's something that looks and tastes very special while still being easy enough for a weeknight. Serve it with hummus and pita for a dinner with Middle Eastern flair. Sumac is a spice with a bright and tangy flavor that goes very well with chicken. I love using rainbow carrots to add extra color, but use whatever you've got access to.

MAKES 4 SERVINGS

SUMAC MIX
¼ cup olive oil
1½ tablespoons sumac
1 tablespoon smoked paprika
½ teaspoon red pepper flakes
1½ teaspoons salt
1 teaspoon ground black pepper
1 teaspoon brown sugar

CHICKEN AND VEGGIES
½ head cauliflower, cut into florets
1 pound rainbow carrots, halved lengthwise
2 pounds bone-in, skin-on chicken legs and thighs
2–3 garlic cloves, thinly sliced
1 small lemon, thinly sliced
1 small red onion, cut into wedges

HERBED OIL
¼ cup chopped parsley
¼ cup chopped cilantro
1 tablespoon za'atar
Juice of ½ lemon
2 tablespoons olive oil

Preheat the oven to 400°F. Line a rimmed baking sheet with parchment paper.

In a small bowl, combine the ingredients for the sumac mix.

Spread out the cauliflower and carrots on the prepared baking sheet and drizzle with half the sumac blend. Stir to coat. In a mixing bowl, pour the remaining half of the sumac mix over the chicken and turn to coat. Place the chicken on the baking sheet with the cauliflower and carrots. Scatter the garlic slices, lemon slices, and onion over the baking sheet.

Roast for 40 to 45 minutes until the vegetables are tender and the chicken is cooked through, turning over the veggies and chicken halfway through.

While the sumac chicken is roasting, mix the ingredients for the herbed oil in a small bowl. Drizzle the oil over the cooked chicken and veggies and serve right away.

CHICKEN AND YELLOW RICE

We love to travel as a family, and it's so fun to bring home my own version of a meal we had on a trip. This one is inspired by the Halal Guys cart in New York City. It's a famous food truck that always has a long line of tourists and locals waiting to enjoy their spiced shawarma chicken and famous yellow rice.

Re-creating this meal at home immediately brings us back to sitting on a park bench in NYC enjoying this delicious dinner as we people watch. Don't forget to top it with the white sauce!

MAKES 6 SERVINGS

CHICKEN AND MARINADE
1 tablespoon paprika
1 tablespoon garlic powder
1 tablespoon ground cumin
1 teaspoon red pepper flakes
1 teaspoon sumac
1½ teaspoons salt
2 teaspoons dried parsley
1 teaspoon za'atar
3 tablespoons lemon juice
4 tablespoons olive oil
6 boneless skin-on chicken
    thighs and legs

RICE
1½ cups basmati rice
1 tablespoon butter
1 teaspoon salt
1 teaspoon ground cumin
½ teaspoon ground turmeric
3 cups water or chicken stock

WHITE SAUCE
½ cup mayonnaise
½ cup yogurt
½ teaspoon sugar
2 tablespoons white vinegar
1 teaspoon lemon juice
¼ cup chopped fresh parsley
Kosher salt and freshly
    ground black pepper
Pinch of paprika

TOPPINGS
Shredded iceberg lettuce
Chopped tomatoes
Hot sauce

In a bowl, combine the marinade ingredients, including 3 tablespoons of the olive oil. Add the chicken and turn to coat. Cover and refrigerate for 30 minutes.

While the chicken is marinating, pour the rice into a bowl and cover with cold water.

When you're ready to cook, heat the remaining 1 tablespoon olive oil in a large, heavy-bottomed pan on medium-high heat. Cook the chicken, skin side down, for 3 to 4 minutes until browned underneath, then flip and brown for 3 to 4 minutes on the other side. Remove the chicken to a plate and set aside.

Away from the heat, wipe out the pan with a paper towel to remove any burnt bits. Return the pan to medium heat and melt the butter. Add the salt, cumin, and turmeric and stir well.

Drain the rice and add it to the pan. Give everything a good stir. Pour in the water and bring to a boil. Add the chicken, then simmer, covered, for 15 minutes. Turn off the heat, but keep the lid on the pan for 5 to 10 minutes.

While your chicken and rice are resting, mix all the white sauce ingredients in a bowl.

Serve with the lettuce, tomatoes, white sauce, and hot sauce.

HANDI CHICKEN

When the kids were younger we went to Jaipur, India, and visited a famous restaurant called Handi. Twice. (It was that good!) When we got back home to Canada, the kids would not stop talking about the chicken we had there. After some research, experimenting, and lots of trial and error, we all felt like I'd nailed it. It's a recipe—and a memory—that I hold near and dear.

MAKES 6 SERVINGS

2 tablespoons vegetable oil
1½ pounds boneless chicken thighs, cut into 1½-inch cubes
1½ tablespoons garlic paste (page 13)
1½ tablespoons ginger paste (page 13)
Salt and pepper to taste
1 medium white onion, finely chopped
2 tablespoons cumin seeds
1½ teaspoons ground red chile
1½ teaspoons ground turmeric
1½ teaspoons ground cumin
1½ teaspoons ground coriander
1½ teaspoons garam masala
1½ teaspoons ground Tandoori Mix (page 19)
2 tomatoes, chopped
2 tablespoons plain yogurt
¼ cup evaporated milk
2 tablespoons tomato paste
1 teaspoon fresh ginger strips
1 medium green chile, chopped
Cilantro, for garnish

Heat 1 tablespoon of the oil in a large pot over medium-high heat. Add the chicken, garlic and ginger pastes, and salt and pepper to taste and fry until the chicken begins to brown on the edges, for 4 to 5 minutes. Remove the chicken pieces and juices and set aside.

In the same pot, heat the remaining 1 tablespoon of oil. Add the onion and all the spices and cook for 2 to 3 minutes until the onion begins to soften and everything is fragrant, then lower the heat to medium. Add the tomatoes and cook until they break down into a sauce, for about 5 minutes. Add the chicken and juices back in, stir, and simmer for 2 to 4 minutes. Add the yogurt, evaporated milk, and tomato paste and cook on low until the sauce comes together, for about 5 minutes.

Top with the ginger, green chile, and cilantro.

ONE-POT CHICKEN PILAU

Every week growing up, we'd come home from Sunday school and my mom would serve up this pilau for lunch. Marinated chicken, tomato, and onion are simmered with rice and flavored with aromatic spices (I remember how it made the whole house smell absolutely amazing!). It's still one of my favorite comfort foods, but these days I like to make it for dinner. It does involve some prep and takes some time to cook, but it's so worth it. Serve with Kachumber (Indian Side Salad) (page 106), Gajar Athano (Pickled Carrots) (page 20), and plain yogurt.

MAKES 8 SERVINGS

CHICKEN AND MARINADE

2 tablespoons plain yogurt
2 teaspoons ground red chile
1 teaspoon ground turmeric
2 tablespoons garlic paste
  (page 13)
1½ tablespoons ginger
  paste (page 13)
2 teaspoons salt
1 tablespoon vegetable oil
3 pounds skinless chicken
  pieces (legs, thighs, and
  breast)

RICE PILAU

2 cups basmati rice
3 tablespoons vegetable oil
2 small cinnamon sticks
3 cardamom pods
7–10 whole peppercorns
4–5 whole cloves
2 teaspoons cumin seeds
2 medium onions, thinly sliced
3–4 medium potatoes, diced
1 small tomato, chopped
1 tablespoon green chutney
  (page 14)
2 teaspoons salt
3–4 cups water
1 teaspoon lemon juice
1½ teaspoons garam masala

In a large bowl, combine the marinade ingredients. Add the chicken and stir until the meat is well coated. Cover and refrigerate for a few hours up to overnight.

Rinse the rice in a mesh strainer till the water runs clear to remove the starch. Transfer the rice to a bowl and cover with cold water. Set aside.

Heat the oil in a large pot over medium-high heat. Add the cinnamon sticks, cardamom pods, peppercorns, cloves, and cumin seeds and toast for a few minutes until fragrant. Add the onions and potatoes. Give everything a good stir and cook until the onion begins to soften and brown, for 3 to 5 minutes. Add the marinated chicken, tomato, chutney, and salt and mix well. Cook for 5 to 6 minutes until the chicken begins to brown.

Drain the rice. Add the water to the chicken mixture and bring to a boil. Add the rice and stir to incorporate everything. Boil until most of the water has evaporated (keep an eye on this). Simmer, then add the lemon juice and garam masala on top of the rice and cover with a lid. Cook for 15 minutes, then turn off the heat. With the lid on the pot, let everything rest for another 8 to 10 minutes.

Just before serving, take the lid off the pot and give everything a good stir from the edges (be gentle so that most of the rice grains will stay whole).

WHOLE TANDOORI CHICKEN

There are a few recipes that you usually hold on to that are perfect for special occasions. This whole tandoori chicken is one of those—it's just so beautiful to serve up to your loved ones. The chicken needs to be spatchcocked (you can ask your butcher to do that for you!) and the recipe requires a little bit of prep and a long marinade time. But after you've marinated your chicken, all you need to do is just pop it into a hot oven and wait for your house to smell amazing!

MAKES 4 SERVINGS

1 cup plain yogurt
1½ tablespoons garlic paste (page 13)
1½ tablespoons ginger paste (page 13)
1 teaspoon ground cumin
1 teaspoon ground coriander
1 teaspoon ground red chile
1 teaspoon ground turmeric
1 teaspoon garam masala
1 teaspoon tandoori mix (page 19)
1 teaspoon salt
1 tablespoon green chutney (page 14)
2 tablespoons chopped cilantro, plus more for garnish
1 tablespoon lemon juice
1 tablespoon neutral oil
1 (3½–4 pound) whole chicken, spatchcocked

In a small bowl, combine all the ingredients except the chicken and mix well.

Place the chicken in a shallow bowl or baking dish. Cover it with the marinade and be sure to massage it into every little nook and cranny! It will make the chicken more tender. Cover and place in the fridge for 6 to 12 hours.

When you're ready to cook, line a rimmed baking sheet with parchment paper. Transfer the chicken to the baking sheet and let it come to room temperature, for 30 to 45 minutes. Preheat the oven to 425°F.

Roast the chicken for 20 minutes, then lower the heat to 375°F and roast for another 40 minutes, basting with pan juices every 20 minutes, until the chicken reaches an internal temperature of 165°F. Remove the chicken from the oven and allow it to rest for 10 minutes, then garnish with cilantro and serve. I like serving this dish with Kachumber (Indian Side Salad) (page 106) and Quinoa Herb Salad (page 109).

CHICKEN SOUVLAKI WRAPS

I often marinate a large batch of this chicken and freeze it so I have it ready to grill up anytime I need a quick dinner plan. These wraps are great for families—especially ones with picky eaters—because everyone can add the toppings they like. And best of all, the leftovers will make a great lunch the next day. Try it on a Greek salad!

MAKES 6 SERVINGS

CHICKEN AND MARINADE

1 small yellow onion, chopped
1½ tablespoons olive oil, plus more for cooking
1 cup plain Greek yogurt
⅓ cup lemon juice
4–5 garlic cloves, minced
1 teaspoon salt
1 teaspoon ground black pepper
2½ teaspoons paprika
2½ teaspoons ground cumin
1 teaspoon red pepper flakes
2 tablespoons dried oregano
6 boneless, skinless chicken breasts, cut in 1-inch cubes

WRAPS

6 pitas
Tzatziki
Olives
Lettuce, thinly sliced
Tomatoes, diced
Cucumbers, diced
Feta cheese
Hot sauce
Fresh parsley

In a large bowl, mix all the marinade ingredients. Add the cubed chicken and stir to coat. Cover and refrigerate for 30 minutes or up to overnight. Or you could put it into airtight freezer bags and freeze it for up to 3 months.

To cook the chicken on the stove, heat vegetable oil in a large cast-iron skillet or frying pan over medium-high heat. Add the chicken and cook, turning occasionally, until browned and cooked through, for 7 to 10 minutes.

To grill the chicken, thread the chicken cubes onto skewers. Heat a grill and cook until golden on the outside and juicy on the inside, for 4 to 5 minutes per side.

Warm the pitas in a toaster or in the oven.

Lay all your toppings out on the table so people can build their wrap the way they like it.

SEEKH KEBABS

When I'm making a dish, it's not only about the taste, the aroma, and the nutritional factor—it's often also about the memories the dish evokes. This recipe takes me right back to being in my room doing homework, getting a whiff from the kitchen, and realizing my mom was making kebabs. I would run down, grab a few hot off the plate, and run back upstairs. She always made extra because she knew my siblings and I would eat half of them even before they made it to the dinner table. These days, I know the second Ahmed and Asiyah smell these kebabs cooking, I'll hear footsteps running to the kitchen to grab a few of the spicy meatballs hot from the stove. If the kebabs make it to the dinner table, I love serving them with roti and topping them with cucumber, thinly sliced onions, ambli, and raita. If the plate is missing a few kebabs, that's just fine with me—Ahmed and Asiyah are my official taste testers, after all!

MAKES 10 LARGE KEBABS OR 20 SMALL ONES

1 large onion, finely diced
2 green chiles, or 1 jalapeño
Handful of cilantro
1 tablespoon garlic paste (page 13)
1 tablespoon ginger paste (page 13)
2 pounds ground beef (I like half lean, half regular)
¼ cup bread crumbs
1½ tablespoons garam masala
2 teaspoons ground red chile
1 teaspoon ground cumin
1 teaspoon ground coriander
1 teaspoon ground turmeric
1½ teaspoons salt
2 tablespoons vegetable oil for pan-frying

Place the onion, green chile, cilantro, and garlic and ginger pastes in a food processor and blend into a chunky paste. Transfer it to a large bowl and add the beef, bread crumbs, spices, and salt and combine everything.

Place the mixture in the fridge, covered, for 1 to 2 hours (this makes it easier to handle).

Line a baking sheet with parchment.

With your hands, shape the beef mixture into ten or twenty disks (like a medium-sized burger pattie) and place them on the prepared baking sheet. If the mixture sticks, wet your hands a little.

To grill the kebabs, heat a grill until very hot and cook for 4 to 5 minutes per side until browned and cooked through.

To broil, place your baking sheet of kebabs on the top rack and broil for 3 to 4 minutes on each side until browned and cooked through (keep an eye on the kebabs; every oven is a little different).

To pan-fry, heat the oil in a frying pan over medium heat. Working in batches, fry the kebabs until browned and cooked through, for 2 to 3 minutes per side. Place them on a plate lined with paper towels to absorb the excess oil.

TIP: No bread crumbs? No problem. Pulse a slice of bread into crumbs in your food processor (you may want to toast it first).

BEEF AND BROCCOLI STIR-FRY

Stir-fries are such a great way to pull together a quick, easy flavor-packed meal. Plus, it's a great way to use veggies in the fridge that you want to finish up. The thin pieces of beef cook up nice and tender, and the broccoli stays a little crisp and soaks up all the sauce. Serve over rice or noodles and everyone is happy!

MAKES 4 SERVINGS

1 tablespoon cornstarch
1 tablespoon soy sauce
1 tablespoon oyster sauce
1 tablespoon sambal oelek
1 teaspoon brown sugar
4 cloves minced garlic
2 teaspoons minced ginger
1 teaspoon ground black
    pepper
1½ pounds thin beef strips
1½ tablespoons sesame oil
1 onion, sliced
1 small head of broccoli, cut
    into florets
1 tablespoon dark soy sauce
Sesame seeds, for garnish
Cilantro, for garnish

In a large bowl, mix the cornstarch with ¼ cup of cold water, then add the soy sauce, oyster sauce, sambal olek, brown sugar, garlic, ginger, and pepper. Add the beef and stir to completely coat.

Heat 1 tablespoon of the sesame oil in a frying pan over high heat. Add the onion and broccoli and cook till the veggies begin to soften, for 2 to 3 minutes. Transfer the vegetables to a plate and set aside.

Heat the remaining ½ tablespoon sesame oil in the same pan and add the beef and marinade. Cook until the beef is browned and the sauce thickens up. Stir in the dark soy sauce, then the veggies, and cook for another 4 to 5 minutes until the sauce coats the broccoli and meat.

Sprinkle the sesame seeds and cilantro on top and serve.

KARAHI GOSHT
(Lamb Karahi)

Karahi Gosht, a lamb curry named after the type of pan it is traditionally prepared in, is a favorite at Indian restaurants. I love to make it at home so that I can control the oil. I'm not going to lie; there is still more oil in this than most other curries, but since this is a once-in-a-while dish, you might as well make sure it's super flavorful. It's easy to make but takes time for the meat to get nice and tender and all the flavors to meld and bloom in this thick tomato sauce. Instead of lamb, you can also make it with veal. I like to choose some pieces of meat with the bone in, which adds even more flavor to your curry.

SERVES 4 GENEROUSLY

3 tablespoons vegetable oil
1 tablespoon butter or ghee
2½ tablespoons minced garlic
2 tablespoons minced ginger
2½ pounds chopped lamb or veal shoulder or stew meat
4 medium tomatoes, finely chopped
2 teaspoons salt
2 teaspoons paprika or ground Kashmiri chile
1 teaspoon ground black pepper
1 teaspoon ground red chile
½ teaspoon ground cumin
½ teaspoon ground coriander
2 tablespoons plain yogurt
½ teaspoon garam masala
2 small green chiles, whole or sliced lengthwise
1 cup chopped cilantro
Ginger, cut into matchsticks for topping
Naan, for serving

Heat the oil and butter in a large pot on high heat. Add the garlic and ginger and cook, stirring, until fragrant. Add the meat and stir to coat; cook until the meat is brown, for 7 to 10 minutes. Add the tomatoes, salt, paprika, pepper, ground red chile, cumin, and coriander and mix well. Stir in ½ cup water. Cover and simmer on low heat for 40 to 45 minutes until the meat is very tender and the oil begins to separate from the sauce. Stir in the yogurt, then add another ½ cup of water, mix, and cook for another 15 minutes. The curry should have a nice, thick consistency. Stir well, adding the garam masala, green chiles, cilantro, and ginger. Serve right away with naan.

INDIAN LAMB CHOPS

My Asiyah is a meat lover. When I tell her I'm making steak, ribs, or lamb chops, her eyes light up! It took me a while to get lamb chops just right, and the trick is the spice rub—the fresher the ground spices, the better. It's so good and can be used for ribs or steak as well. I find my air fryer does the best job, but you could easily grill these or pop them on the BBQ. Serve with Kachumber (Indian Side Salad) (page 106) and naan.

MAKES 4 SERVINGS

SPICE RUB AND LAMB

2–3 tablespoons olive oil
2 teaspoons ground cumin
1 tablespoon ground coriander
½ teaspoon ground nutmeg
2 teaspoons ground turmeric
1–2 teaspoons ground red chile
½ teaspoon ground cardamom
1 teaspoon ground cinnamon
2 teaspoons salt
1 teaspoon ground black pepper
1 teaspoon ginger paste (page 13)
1½ teaspoons garlic paste (page 13)
6–8 lamb chops (about 1½ inches thick)

YOGURT MINT SAUCE

½ cup plain yogurt
1 tablespoon green chutney (page 14)
¼ cup chopped fresh mint
Lemon wedges, for serving

In a large, shallow bowl, combine all the spice rub ingredients. Give everything a good mix.

Coat the lamb chops well on each side with the spice rub. Cover and place in the fridge for 20 to 30 minutes to allow the spices to flavor the meat.

To make the yogurt mint sauce: In a small bowl, mix the yogurt, green chutney, and mint, then set it aside at room temperature.

Preheat the oven to 350°F.

Take the lamb chops out a few minutes before you're ready to cook so they come to room temperature. Heat your grill until it's very hot, or warm a cast-iron skillet over medium-high heat on the stove. Sear the lamb chops for 3 to 4 minutes per side until browned, then finish them off in the oven for 8 to 10 minutes (depending on the thickness of your chops) until the juices run clear and they reach an internal temperature of 140 degrees.

Transfer the lamb to a plate and cover it lightly with foil. Allow it to rest for 5 minutes before serving with the lemon wedges and yogurt mint sauce.

CELEBRATION LEG OF LAMB

Every family has that one star dish—the centerpiece to a celebration dinner that everyone loves. This leg of lamb is my mom's pride and joy. And, man, is it a beauty. If you've never made one before, this recipe may seem intimidating, but think of it like roasting a turkey or a whole chicken. There's a little prep, but most of the work is done in the oven. The meat is cooked to falling-off-the-bone perfection and then grilled and topped with a saucy tomato gravy. Serve it with naan or paratha, roasted potatoes, and a green salad. My mouth waters just thinking about it!

MAKES 10 SERVINGS

LAMB AND YOGURT SAUCE

1 cup plain yogurt
4 tablespoons garlic paste (page 13)
4 tablespoons ginger paste (page 13)
3 tablespoons vegetable oil
2 tablespoons green chutney (page 14)
3 teaspoons salt
2 teaspoons ground black pepper
2 teaspoons ground coriander
2 teaspoons ground cumin
1 (5- to 7-pound) bone-in leg of lamb

TOMATO SAUCE

2 cups crushed tomatoes
2 tablespoons tomato paste
2–3 teaspoons ground red chile
1 tablespoon green chutney (page 14)
2 teaspoons salt
1 tablespoon butter
1½ teaspoons garam masala
¼ cup chopped cilantro, for garnish

Preheat the oven to 350°F.

In a bowl, mix the yogurt, garlic and ginger pastes, vegetable oil, green chutney, salt, pepper, coriander, and cumin for the yogurt sauce.

Place the lamb in a large, ovenproof dish and, with kitchen scissors or a sharp knife, make a few inch-deep cuts into the flesh of the lamb to allow the marinade to penetrate and the lamb to cook more evenly. Pour the yogurt sauce over the lamb and massage it into the meat to evenly coat. Cover the lamb with foil and place in the oven. Cook for 3½ to 4 hours until the meat easily pulls off the bone. Remove the pan from the oven and pour off the juices into a saucepan. Place the lamb back into the oven uncovered and cook for another 15 minutes.

Meanwhile, set the saucepan with the pan juices on the stove over medium-high heat. Add the crushed tomatoes, tomato paste, ground red chile, green chutney, and salt and give it a stir. Allow the mixture to come to a simmer and thicken up. Add the butter to give the sauce a silky texture and finish off with garam masala. The sauce should be a dark, rich red color.

Pour the tomato sauce over the cooked lamb and place back in the oven on the bottom rack to broil for 5 to 7 minutes. This will brown the meat and bring the flavors together.

Remove the lamb from the oven and allow it to rest for 5 to 10 minutes. Top with cilantro.

MANY OF MY LUNCH AND DINNER RECIPES ARE
one-and-done style, which I know we all appreciate.
Some meals, however, do benefit from sides. And
sometimes, sides are substantial enough to be a meal
on their own! Whether you're looking for something
to pair up with a main dish or a lighter meal or snack,
this chapter has plenty of options for you. Some of
these recipes could be bought at the store, such as
naan or roti or guacamole. I promise you, though,
once you go homemade, you won't go back! I hope
you'll give them a try!

SIMPLE GUACAMOLE

Some dishes are delicious enough to serve for company and yet so simple your kids can make them. This is one of those recipes for us. It was the first entry my daughter wrote in the little notebook where she keeps her favorite recipes. A few years later, she still refers back to it, even though she's made it dozens of times! Everyone has their preference, but we love ours spicy and chunky with loads of garlic and lime! Don't forget that guacamole is more than just a dip—add it to tacos, eggs, burgers, sandwiches—the list goes on.

MAKES 3 TO 4 CUPS

4 ripe avocados, peeled and pitted
½ red onion, finely chopped
1 small tomato, chopped (optional)
1 jalapeño, chopped (optional)
2 garlic cloves, minced
Juice of 2 limes
½ cup chopped cilantro
½ teaspoon salt
½ teaspoon ground cumin

Combine all the ingredients in a large bowl. Mash the avocados while stirring to incorporate everything together. How thoroughly you mash is really up to you, depending on how chunky or smooth you (or your loved ones!) like guacamole to be.

Store any leftover guacamole in an airtight container in the fridge for up to 2 days.

PINEAPPLE SALSA

This salsa's sweet, tangy, and spicy combination is a riot of flavor. It's a perfect side for a picnic or a BBQ. It also goes great with nachos, grilled chicken, or fish tacos! If you don't have a food processor, you can still make this recipe; simply chop the fruit, vegetables, and cilantro very finely by hand.

MAKES 2 CUPS

1½ cups pineapple chunks
¼ cup roughly chopped red onion
¼ cup roughly chopped red pepper
½ large jalapeño (remove the seeds if you want it less spicy)
¼ bunch cilantro
1½ tablespoons olive oil
Juice of 1 lime
½ teaspoon crushed red pepper
½ teaspoon sugar
½ teaspoon salt

Put all your ingredients in a food processor. Slowly pulse in 1- to 2-second increments until the ingredients have reached a fine consistency and are well combined (but not puréed—stop processing before you end up with juice!).

Transfer the salsa into a serving bowl.

Store any leftovers in an airtight container in the fridge for up to 4 days.

MANGO AVOCADO SALSA

This luscious yet refreshing salsa is so versatile, you'll find yourself putting it on everything. It's great spooned onto grilled chicken or fish, adds kick to a sandwich, and makes an addictive dip with toasted pita. The only downside is that it disappears way too fast!

MAKES 4 CUPS

Juice of ½ lime
1 tablespoon olive oil
2 teaspoons Tajín spice (you can make your own with equal parts salt, sugar, and chili powder)
2 mangoes, peeled and cut into 1-inch cubes
1 avocado, peeled and cut into 1-inch cubes
½ red onion, finely chopped
½ red bell pepper, finely chopped
2 tablespoons chopped cilantro

In a small bowl, whisk the lime juice, olive oil, and spices.

Add the rest of the ingredients and gently toss until everything is combined.

Serve the salsa immediately or place in an airtight container and store in the fridge for up to 3 days.

BASIC ROTI

Every culture has its version of flatbread, and Indian cuisine has many. Roti is one of my absolute faves. Growing up, I loved grabbing a fresh roti off the stove just as my mom was finished making them. It was so mesmerizing watching her do three things nearly at once—rolling out the dough for one roti and then flipping the other one cooking on the stove while finishing off the curry we were going to eat, all in one sweeping motion. Today, as I'm trying to match her roti-making game, I think about the motions she makes, how she rolls and flips the dough. There's a joke that the sign of a good cook is how round their rotis are. My mom's are circular perfection. At first mine admittedly resembled continents more than circles, but slowly, with practice, they've actually gotten pretty decent! The key I find is to rotate the roti as you're rolling it out. I make mine with whole wheat flour, giving them a nice brown color.

Serve them with your favorite curry, use them as wraps for kebabs or eggs, or simply top them with a little butter and either jam or sugar and dip in your tea!

MAKES 10 TO 12 ROTIS

---

2 ¼ cups whole wheat flour
1½ tablespoons vegetable oil
¾ cup warm water, plus more as needed for kneading
2 tablespoons ghee or melted butter

Measure 2 cups of the flour into a large mixing bowl. Pour in the oil and mix it into the flour using your fingertips. Slowly add the water bit by bit, gently mixing with your fingers to bring together the dough. Once it starts to come together, you may need to adjust the ingredients. If the dough seems too dry, add a little more water (a tablespoon at a time), and if it seems too sticky, add a little more flour. Keep kneading with your hands and applying pressure with your palms to mix and flatten until the dough is soft and pliable.

Let the dough rest, covered with a tea towel, for 20 to 30 minutes.

Knead the dough again for 1 to 2 minutes until you have a soft and pliable but not sticky dough.

Spread out the remaining ¼ cup flour on a plate. Separate the dough into ten to twelve equal balls.

Heat a frying pan or tawa on high heat.

One by one, roll each ball between your hands and flatten into a circle.

Dip a flattened dough ball into the flour to coat both sides. On a flat surface, roll out the dough with a rolling pin to a thin circle 5 to 6 inches in diameter, turning occasionally and applying a little pressure to flatten the dough. If the roti is sticking to the rolling pin or surface below, dust with a little more flour.

Place one roti on the pan. Cook for 30 seconds, then flip right away with a wooden spatula or your fingers (the first flip is always quick!). Cook a little longer on the second side until the roti has brown spots underneath, then flip over one last time. When you press down on the roti with a flat spatula for flipping, it will puff up. Transfer the cooked roti from the pan to a plate and brush with a little ghee or butter. Cover it with a clean dish towel to keep it warm. Repeat the rolling/cooking/brushing process with the remaining dough balls until all the rotis are cooked.

Rotis are best eaten right away.

FRESH NAAN

Unlike roti (see page 192), naan is a leavened flatbread, making it a bit thicker and chewier. Naan is perfect for scooping up all those delicious curries and almost as good when you use it as a wrap. Or if you're like my kids, you just might eat yours fresh off the stove all on its own.

MAKES 6 NAANS

2½ cups all-purpose flour
1 tablespoon sugar
1 teaspoon instant dry yeast
½ teaspoon baking soda
½ teaspoon salt
½ cup plain yogurt
3 tablespoons plus 1 teaspoon vegetable oil
½ cup lukewarm water
2–3 tablespoons ghee or butter
1–2 garlic cloves, minced
1 tablespoon finely chopped cilantro

In a large mixing bowl, combine 2 cups of the flour with the sugar, yeast, baking soda, and salt and stir to incorporate. Add the yogurt and 3 tablespoons of the oil and mix into the flour with a spoon. Gradually pour in the water and stir until a dough starts to form. Lightly flour your hands and knead to keep bringing the dough together; it will be a shaggy, imperfect ball, and that's okay! Lightly oil a large clean bowl and transfer your dough into it. Cover with a kitchen towel and let sit for 30 minutes.

Tip the dough out onto a lightly floured work surface. With a little more flour on your hands, knead the dough into a large soft ball. It won't take very long, about 30 seconds.

Separate the dough into six equal sections and roll each one into a small ball. With a rolling pin, roll out each ball of dough into an oval shape.

In a small bowl, stir together 1½ tablespoons of melted ghee, minced garlic, and cilantro. Set aside.

Melt a small amount (about 1 teaspoon) of ghee in a large, heavy-bottomed pan or cast-iron skillet over medium-high heat. Add one of the naans and cook for about 1 minute until you see air bubbles forming on the top. Flip the naan and cook for another 1 to 2 minutes until golden brown in some spots. Remove the cooked naan to a plate.

Brush the butter and garlic mixture over each naan as it comes off the pan.

Repeat the cooking/brushing process for the rest of the naan. Serve warm.

BROCCOLI FRITTERS

Broccoli and cheese? Yes, please! These bites will get even the pickiest eater eating their veggies. They are great to serve alongside Baked Chicken Nuggets (page 81), Mean Green Tuna Salad Sandwich (page 61), or anytime you want to add some green to your meal.

MAKES 12 TO 15 FRITTERS

2½ cups chopped broccoli
1 cup shredded Cheddar cheese
¾ cup almond meal or panko bread crumbs
½ small onion, chopped
⅓ cup chopped cilantro
2 eggs
1 teaspoon red pepper flakes
Salt and pepper to taste
4 teaspoons olive oil

Steam the broccoli until very soft. Transfer it to a large bowl and smash with a fork until well mashed (a little more texture than mashed potatoes). Let it cool to room temperature.

Add the remaining ingredients except for the oil and mix everything until well combined. With a tablespoon, measure the broccoli mixture and make into little patties.

Heat the oil in a frying pan over medium heat. Working in batches, drop the broccoli patties into the oil. Cook on one side until they begin to turn golden, for 2 to 3 minutes, then flip and cook on the other side for another 2 minutes more. Transfer to a paper towel–lined plate and repeat with the remaining broccoli mixture. Serve hot.

CRISPY MASALA ROASTED POTATOES

Potatoes are always a good idea—the perfect side to just about any dish, and especially good with my Whole Tandoori Chicken (page 172) or Celebration Leg of Lamb (page 182). That warm and cozy feeling you get when you bite into a perfectly cooked potato is magic! These potatoes are boiled first to ensure they're cooked through and keep their insides soft. Then they take a dip in a masala spice mixture to give them a pop of flavor and are finished off in the oven, where they crisp up beautifully.

MAKES 4 SERVINGS

3 teaspoons salt
3 pounds small potatoes, halved
2 tablespoons olive oil
1 tablespoon butter
1 garlic clove, minced
1 teaspoon ground coriander
1 teaspoon cumin seeds
1 teaspoon red pepper flakes
½ teaspoon ground turmeric
½ teaspoon ground red chile
½ teaspoon paprika
½ teaspoon onion powder
Chopped cilantro, for garnish
Plain yogurt, for serving (optional)

Preheat the oven to 350°F.

Bring a large pot of water to a boil and put in 2 teaspoons of the salt. Add the potatoes. Cook for 10 minutes or until fork-tender. Drain well.

In the meantime, in an ovenproof baking dish, combine the oil, butter, garlic, and all the spices. Add your potatoes and gently toss to coat with spices. Bake for 18 to 20 minutes until the potatoes are fully cooked and crispy on the outside. Remove from the oven and top with the cilantro.

Serve with yogurt.

JEERA RICE WITH MIXED VEGETABLES

Rice is a standard in so many households, and ours is no different. I love how such a simple ingredient can be cooked in so many different ways! This recipe makes an excellent accompaniment to your favorite curry, or my Whole Tandoori Chicken (page 172) or Celebration Leg of Lamb (page 182). But because of the warm, earthy flavor of the jeera (cumin) and the addition of vegetables, my kids often eat it with yogurt, and sometimes that's their whole meal! Simple and delicious.

MAKES 6 SERVINGS

2 cups basmati rice
1 tablespoon vegetable oil
   or butter
1 teaspoon cumin seeds
2 teaspoons salt
1 teaspoon garlic paste
   (page 13)
¾ cup frozen mixed
   vegetables, thawed
1¾ cups water

Rinse the rice in a mesh strainer. Pour it into a large bowl, cover it with cold water, and soak for 30 minutes at room temperature.

In a large pot, heat the oil on medium heat. Add the cumin seeds and toast until fragrant, for about 1 minute. Add the salt and garlic paste and stir well until the garlic is golden.

Add the mixed vegetables and stir to incorporate everything. Stir in the drained soaked rice. Pour in the water. Bring the pot to a boil, then simmer, covered, for 12 minutes. Turn off the heat and allow the pot to sit, covered, for another 5 minutes.

Remove the lid and fluff up the rice with a fork. Serve hot.

Chicken Veggie Spring Rolls, p. 203

Dhokra, p. 202

Bhajia, p. 201

BHAJIA
(Mung Bean Fritters)

Bhajia are one of my daughter's favorites. My mom makes sure to have a fresh batch anytime Asiyah visits. A sort of Indian fritter, they're a great vegetarian side dish, made out of mung beans, cilantro, chiles, and some spices, all deep-fried to perfection, with a crispy outside and soft fluffy inside. They also make an amazing topping for a curry like Chana Bateta (page 80).

MAKES 25 TO 30 BHAJIA

1 cup yellow split mung beans (moong dal)
2 cups split black-eyed peas
1 small onion, chopped
1½ teaspoons garlic paste (page 13)
2 green chiles
1½ teaspoons salt
2 tablespoons chopped cilantro
½ teaspoon Eno or baking soda (see Tip)
Vegetable oil for frying
Coconut chutney (page 16), for serving

Rinse the beans and peas in a mesh strainer several times to remove the husks and until the water runs clear. Tip the beans into a large bowl and cover with cold water. Soak overnight in the fridge to soften. Drain.

In a food processor, combine the beans, peas, onion, garlic paste, green chiles, and salt and pulse until well combined (like a lumpy pancake batter). Pour the mixture into a bowl. Add the cilantro and Eno and mix well with a fork to fluff up the mixture.

Pour the oil into a large skillet to about 4 inches deep and heat over medium heat.

Working in batches, take a heaping tablespoon of the mixture and shape it into a small ball, then drop it into the oil. Fry the bhajia on both sides till golden brown all over. Transfer the cooked bhajia to a paper towel–lined plate. Serve hot with the coconut chutney.

TIP: Eno is a fruit salt sold as an antacid and comes in different flavors. It is sometimes used like baking powder in Indian cooking. If you don't have Eno, baking soda will do!

DHOKRA

This is a beautiful appetizer to serve up when guests come over. Think of it as an Indian savory sponge cake. Originating from the Gujarat state of India, dhokra is made primarily with semolina and chickpea flour, lightened with yogurt, and topped with a mixture of tempered whole spices called wagar. It's steamed rather than baked to create a light, fluffy texture.

MAKES 1 CAKE OF 8 TO 10 PIECES

1 cup semolina flour (soji)
2 tablespoons chickpea flour
2 tablespoons chopped cilantro
1 teaspoon salt
¼ teaspoon ground turmeric
1¼ cups yogurt
¾ cup hot water
2 tablespoons lemon juice
1 teaspoon garlic paste (page 13)
3 tablespoons canola oil
1 teaspoon white vinegar
1 teaspoon Eno or baking soda (see Tip on page 201)
1 teaspoon ground red chile

TOPPING (WAGAR)

1 teaspoon black mustard seeds
1 teaspoon cumin seeds
6–8 curry leaves
1 green chile, chopped
Ambli, for serving (optional)

In a large mixing bowl, combine the flours, cilantro, salt, turmeric, yogurt, water, lemon juice, garlic paste, and 2 tablespoons of the oil. Stir well; the batter should be thin and a nice light yellow or golden color. Set aside for 10 to 15 minutes.

Grease an 8-inch round baking pan with oil. Fill a large pot with water to about 2 inches deep. Add the white vinegar. Fit the pot with a steel rack or steaming ring or a legged trivet and place the greased pan on top to heat. Bring the water to a boil.

Add the Eno to your batter; you will see it activate and begin to bubble and fluff up the batter. Mix well with a whisk so that everything is well incorporated (it should be a thick batter consistency, like pancake batter). Carefully remove the baking pan from your steamer pot and immediately pour the batter into the hot greased baking pan. Place the pan into the pot of boiling water. Cover with a heavy lid (make sure there is a tight seal) and steam for 15 minutes until the dhokra has firmed up and cooked through but is still a little spongy.

Remove the pan from the pot and sprinkle the top with ground red chile.

To make the topping (wagar) mixture, heat the remaining 1 tablespoon of oil in a shallow frying pan over medium-high heat. Add the mustard seeds and cumin seeds. Once they begin to crackle, add the curry leaves and green chile and toast for 1 to 2 minutes. Remove from the heat. Spoon the spices over the top of the dhokra.

Cut the dhokra into squares. Serve warm or at room temperature with ambli, if desired.

CHICKEN VEGGIE SPRING ROLLS

These crispy spring rolls take a little time and effort, but the way my family appreciates them (and devours them) makes it so worth it. My favorite time to make these is during Ramadan. Everyone is fasting, so the kids are eager to eat some of their favorites—and I'm happy because they're packed with protein and veggies. It's a win-win!

MAKES ABOUT 15 ROLLS

1 tablespoon garlic paste (page 13)

1 tablespoon ginger paste (page 13)

1 teaspoon green chutney (page 14)

1 teaspoon salt

1 teaspoon ground black pepper

2½ pounds boneless, skinless chicken breasts

1 cup shredded red cabbage

1 large bell pepper, cut into thin strips

1 cup shredded carrots

⅓ cup chopped onion

½ cup frozen corn

½ cup chopped cilantro

1 teaspoon ground red chile

1 teaspoon ground cumin

1 teaspoon ground black pepper

2 tablespoons soy sauce

15 wrappers (wanton or spring roll wrappers, very thin squares of dough)

1 tablespoon flour

Canola oil, for frying

In a large bowl, combine the garlic and ginger pastes, green chutney, salt, and pepper. Add the chicken breasts and turn to coat them thoroughly.

Add the chicken to an Instant Pot. Lock the lid into place and set to sealing. Cook on high pressure for 8 minutes until cooked through. Release the pressure naturally for 10 minutes, then manually release the remaining pressure, press CANCEL, and open the lid. Transfer the chicken to a plate and let it rest until it's cool enough to handle. Shred the chicken using two forks to pull the meat into small pieces.

In a large bowl, toss together all the veggies, herbs, spices, and soy sauce. Add the shredded chicken and combine well with the vegetables.

If you plan to bake your spring rolls, heat the oven to 425°F.

To assemble the spring rolls, unwrap the spring roll packet and wrap it loosely in a damp tea towel or paper towel as you work, to keep the wrappers from drying out. Stir together the flour with 2 tablespoons of water in a small bowl.

Place a wrapper on your work surface so one of the corners is pointing toward you (it should look like a diamond). Spoon about 1½ tablespoons of the filling mixture onto the wrapper near that corner. Roll the corner over the filling once. Gently press the sides of the wrapper to flatten and fold them over the filling. Lightly brush the opposite corner with the flour slurry. Roll the spring roll the rest of the way and press the corner to seal. Repeat with the remaining wrappers and filling.

To fry the spring rolls, fill a skillet with oil to about 2 inches deep. Heat over medium-high heat. Working in batches so as not to crowd the pan, fry the spring rolls for 2 to 3 minutes on each

(Continued)

side until they're golden brown. Transfer the fried rolls to a paper towel–lined plate.

To bake the spring rolls, preheat the oven to 350°F. Place a wire rack in a baking dish and arrange the spring rolls on the rack. Bake for 10 minutes until golden on top, then flip and bake for 8 to 10 minutes more until crisp.

To air-fry the spring rolls, heat your air fryer to 390°F for 3 minutes. Spray the fryer basket with oil. Arrange the spring rolls in the basket, leaving a little space between them, and spray or brush with oil. Air-fry for 9 minutes. The egg rolls should be crispy and lightly browned.

SPICED EGGPLANT

Looking for a great side dish that could easily be eaten as a main? Eggplant is so meaty and filling, and the spicy sauce in this recipe really makes it sing. It's a great dish to serve up at a BBQ; just throw the eggplant on the grill, add the sauce, and voilà!

MAKES 4 SERVINGS

¼ cup tomato purée
1 tablespoon garlic paste (page 13)
1 teaspoon salt
1 teaspoon ground red chile
½ teaspoon ground cumin
½ teaspoon ground coriander
½ teaspoon ground turmeric
½ tablespoon lemon juice
2 large eggplants, cut lengthwise, with cut sides scored with shallow crisscross cuts
1½ tablespoons olive oil
Chopped cilantro, for garnish
Plain yogurt, for garnish (optional)

In a medium bowl, stir together the tomato purée, garlic paste, salt, spices, and lemon juice. Set aside.

Brush the cut sides of the eggplants with the oil.

Heat a grill on medium-high, or an oven-safe frying pan over medium-high heat on the stove. Place the eggplant cut side down on the grill or pan and cook for 10 to 12 minutes until the eggplant is soft and the tip of a knife can easily poke through.

Heat the oven to a low broil. Flip over the eggplant and place it on a baking tray, then brush the tomato sauce on the cut side of the eggplant. Transfer the eggplant to the oven on a rack in the lower third. Broil the eggplant for 2 to 3 minutes (each broiler is different, so keep an eye on it). The sauce should be slightly brown.

Place the cooked eggplant on a serving tray. Sprinkle with cilantro and drizzle with plain yogurt if desired.

CURRIED ROASTED CAULIFLOWER

If you can't get your kids to eat veggies, try this recipe! Cauliflower is a great blank canvas and takes on the flavor of whatever spices or other ingredients you cook it with, so feel free to play around with different combos. This curry spice combo makes the kitchen smell divine, and you can definitely adjust the spice factor to suit your family.

MAKES 4 SERVINGS

2 tablespoons olive oil
2 teaspoons curry powder
1 teaspoon salt
2 teaspoons red pepper
  flakes
1 teaspoon ground turmeric
1 teaspoon paprika
¼ cup chopped cilantro
1 head cauliflower, chopped
  into florets

Preheat the oven to 425°F.

In a large bowl, mix everything except the cauliflower into a paste. Add the cauliflower and toss to evenly coat with all the spices. I like to use my hands—it's okay to get them a little messy!

Spread the cauliflower over two rimmed baking sheets. Allow space in between the florets so that they don't steam.

Roast the cauliflower for 20 to 25 minutes until browned and crispy, flipping the florets halfway through. Serve hot.

Curried Roasted
Cauliflower, p. 206

Spiced Eggplant, p. 205

DRINKS

HERE ARE DRINKS FOR EVERY SEASON AND every reason. There's a latte to rev you up in the morning and an herbal tea to wind you down at night, a fruity refresher to cool you down and a spicy shot to warm you up, and even a healthy elixir shot for when you're feeling under the weather.

GINGER TURMERIC HERBAL TEA

You know when you're feeling under the weather and all you want is your mom, a big comfy couch, and a warm, fuzzy blanket to wrap up in? Nothing beats a hug from your mom, but the warm feeling of drinking this tea might be the next best thing. It's a mix of simple ingredients that you might already have on hand, and the combination is a healing concoction that will instantly make you feel better.

MAKES 4 SERVINGS

4 ½ cups water
1 lemon, sliced (6–8 pieces)
1 (1½-inch) turmeric root, cut into small pieces
1 (1½-inch) ginger root, cut into small pieces
Pinch of ground black pepper
2 tablespoons honey
Fresh mint (optional)

Pour the water into a medium saucepan. Put in the lemon slices, turmeric and ginger pieces, and pepper. Bring to a boil, stirring occasionally. The water will begin to change to a beautiful yellow-golden color. Simmer for 4 to 5 minutes to let the flavors infuse.

Turn off the heat. Pour the tea into cups or a teapot, using a strainer to catch the lemon, ginger, and turmeric. Add some honey and mint, if using, to each individual cup, stir, sip, and enjoy!

TIP: Heating honey too high for too long can cause it to lose some of its health benefits, so stir it into your tea after boiling.

WATERMELON REFRESHER

Want to taste summer in a glass? This fresh and not-too-sweet drink is just that. Perfect for picnics and BBQs, this will definitely be a regular on your summer rotation.

¼ large, seedless watermelon, cut into chunks
8–10 strawberries, hulled
6–8 large mint leaves, roughly chopped
4 cups coconut water
Juice of 1 lime
1 cup ice

Toss everything into your blender and give it a good whiz.

You can keep it in the fridge for 1 to 2 days—you'll want to give it a shake before serving in case it separates.

ENERGY-BOOSTING GREEN SMOOTHIE

My love of smoothies runs deep, so I had to share my all-time favorite here with you! It's just the drink you need when you're looking to boost your energy. It's packed with all the goodness of a bunch of leafy greens, sweetened with apple and pear, and has a nice kick from fresh lemon.

MAKES ABOUT 4 CUPS

1 orange, peeled and
   chopped
2 cups coconut water
1½ cups chopped kale
   leaves
1 cup spinach leaves
1 small cucumber, chopped
½ ripe pear, chopped
½ green apple, chopped
1 tablespoon fresh mint
1 tablespoon cilantro or
   parsley, chopped
Juice of 1 lemon
Small piece of ginger (about
   1 inch thick), peeled and
   chopped
Pinch of ground cayenne
1 cup ice
1–2 cups water

In a high-powered blender, place the orange with the coconut water and purée until smooth. Add the remaining ingredients except the water and blend on high for 20 to 30 seconds until smooth. Pour in enough water to reach your desired consistency. (If there's foam at the top, spoon it out and discard it.) Enjoy the juice right away or pour into jars with a tight lid to keep in the fridge for up to 3 days.

TURMERIC GINGER SHOTS

A shot a day keeps the doctor away! You may have seen these immune-boosting shots in health-food stores or juice bars, but it's really easy to whip up a batch on your own. Organic ginger is best here as you don't need to peel it (but do give it a good scrub). This recipe makes a little more than 5 cups. Extra shots can be stored in a glass container in the fridge.

MAKES ABOUT 5 CUPS (18 SHOTS)

3 large ginger roots, roughly chopped (about 1 cup of ginger)
2 cups filtered water
2 large lemons, peeled
2 oranges, peeled
1 tablespoon honey
2 teaspoons ground turmeric
½ teaspoon cayenne
¼ teaspoon ground black pepper

Scrub the ginger and place in a high-powered blender with the water. Purée until smooth. Strain the ginger juice through a fine-mesh sieve to remove the pulp and return the juice to the blender. Add the lemons, oranges, honey, turmeric, cayenne, and pepper. Blend until well combined. The texture will be similar to a thick juice. Pour into small jars (about 2 ounces per serving).

Store any extra liquid in a glass container in the fridge for up to a week.

MANGO LASSI

If you've been to an Indian or Pakistani restaurant, you've probably noticed this popular drink on the menu. It's the perfect pairing to cool your taste buds down after all the spicy food. It's such a treat and really simple to make at home! If you can find them, Alphonso mangoes are particularly nice here.

MAKES 4 SERVINGS

2 cups pitted, peeled, and
   chopped very ripe mango
1 cup Greek yogurt
1½ cups milk
1 scoop vanilla ice cream
Dash of ground cardamom
1 cup ice

In a blender, add all the ingredients and purée until smooth. Serve immediately.

TURMERIC MILK
(Haldi Doodh)

In many families and cultures there are healing remedies that are passed on from generation to generation. This haldi doodh, or turmeric milk, is a warm drink we make for someone who is feeling under the weather. Each family has a slightly different variation. I love to add cinnamon and saffron to round out all the flavors.

MAKES 1 SERVING

1 cup milk
½ teaspoon ground turmeric
⅓ teaspoon ground cinnamon
¼ teaspoon grated fresh ginger
Pinch saffron
1 tablespoon honey
Pinch of ground black pepper

Pour the milk into a small saucepan set over low heat. Whisk in the turmeric, cinnamon, ginger, and saffron. Right before the milk comes to a boil, remove from the heat and pour into a large cup. Stir in the honey and sprinkle with a very small pinch of black pepper.

MASALA CHAI
(Spiced Tea)

The warm and spiced flavor of a good cup of chai can melt all the world's problems away! Well . . . maybe not, but it certainly helps.

This traditional masala chai is made with simple whole spices boiled with black tea, milk, and sugar. Use your preferred brand of tea—my go-to is Tetley Orange Pekoe. My twist is to add some delicate saffron. This adds such depth of flavor and gives it a beautiful golden hue. Enjoy it after a hearty meal (ginger and spice can aid digestion) or with biscuits or cookies as an afternoon pick-me-up.

MAKES 4 CUPS

5 cups water
3 cardamom pods, crushed
1 cinnamon stick
1-inch piece fresh ginger, peeled and grated
Pinch of saffron strands
3 black tea bags
½ cup evaporated milk
4 teaspoons sugar, or to taste

In a saucepan, bring the water to a boil. Add the cardamom pods, cinnamon stick, ginger, and saffron strands. Simmer for 2 to 3 minutes to infuse the flavors. Add the tea bags to the pan and simmer for an additional 5 minutes.

Pour in the milk and sugar, and stir well. Bring the mixture to a gentle boil.

Then simmer the chai for another 4 to 5 minutes to allow the flavors to blend.

Remove the saucepan from the heat and strain the chai into cups or a teapot. Serve hot.

COCONUT LATTE

As much as I love coffee, I don't drink it every day. It's more of a special occasion kind of thing. I love having a cup over a chat with friends, and this recipe is one special treat to share over a lively conversation. I also love that I don't need an espresso machine to make this café-worthy latte at home. It's so good you'll never believe it's made with instant coffee. It's got healthy fats from coconut oil and a boost of flavor from the cinnamon.

MAKES 2 SERVINGS

2 cups milk (I like to use coconut or the Cashew Milk on page 225)
2 teaspoons instant coffee
1 tablespoon coconut sugar
2 teaspoons coconut oil
½ teaspoon vanilla extract
Dash of ground cinnamon

In a saucepan on medium-high heat, warm the milk until hot but not boiling.

In a large, high-powered blender, place the instant coffee, coconut sugar, coconut oil, and vanilla.

Pour the hot milk into the blender and close the lid. Place a towel over the lid to protect your hand and avoid any heat or liquid splattering. Blend on high for 30 seconds until the coffee is dissolved and the milk becomes frothy.

Pour into your favorite cups, sprinkle with cinnamon, and enjoy!

CASHEW MILK, HEMP MILK, AND OAT MILK

I never thought I'd be the type of person who made her own alternative milks. I would always just grab a carton at the grocery store or pour some in my coffee at a café. But once I tried making my own and realized just how easy and economical it was, I was sold. Each of these milks literally takes a few minutes to make, and then you have a great milk alternative ready in the fridge for the next few days. Making your own also means you can skip the refined sugar and food gums in store-bought nondairy milk. If your milk starts to separate in the fridge, just give it a good shake.

A few ingredients change depending on what type of milk you choose, but the basic idea is the same: combine, blend, pour, and enjoy.

CASHEW MILK

MAKES ABOUT 4 CUPS

1 cup raw cashews
2 whole dates, pitted
Pinch of sea salt
½ teaspoon vanilla extract
4 cups water

In a small bowl, cover the cashews with cold water and soak for 3 to 4 hours. Rinse the cashews with clean water. Transfer to a high-powered blender and add the dates, salt, vanilla, and water. Blend on high for 45 to 60 seconds until creamy, smooth, and frothy. Pour into a large jug/jar that can be sealed.

The milk will keep in the fridge for up to 3 days.

TIP: Cashew milk is perfect for smoothies, coffee, and lattes, or to enjoy over granola.

(Continued)

HEMP MILK

MAKES ABOUT 4 CUPS

½ cup hulled hemp hearts
2 whole dates, pitted
Pinch of sea salt
½ teaspoon vanilla extract
3–4 cups water (see Tip)

Place the hemp hearts, dates, salt, and vanilla in a high-powered blender and pour in the water. Blend on high for 45 to 60 seconds until creamy, smooth, and frothy. Pour into a large jug/jar that can be sealed.

The milk will keep in the fridge for up to 3 days.

TIP: Use less water for thicker, creamier milk! Hemp milk is perfect for smoothies, coffee, and lattes, or to enjoy over granola.

OAT MILK

MAKES ABOUT 4 CUPS

1 cup rolled oats
2 whole dates, pitted
Pinch of sea salt
½ teaspoon vanilla extract
4 cups water

Place the oats, dates, salt, and vanilla in a high-powered blender and add the water. Blend on high for 45 to 60 seconds until creamy, smooth, and frothy. Strain the milk through a fine-mesh strainer or cheesecloth into a large jug/jar that can be sealed.

The milk will keep in the fridge for up to 3 days.

TIP: Oat milk is best enjoyed chilled because it will thicken if heated, but you can add to smoothies, cereal, and granola, and enjoy a little in a cup of coffee.

Cashew Milk,
p. 225

Oat Milk,
p. 226

Hemp Milk,
p. 226

SNACKS & TREATS

TREATS ARE NONNEGOTIABLE IN OUR HOME.

Of course, we all want to eat a healthy diet, but I believe in balance above all—and that means snacks and treats are a part of that healthy and balanced life. We need the recipes that celebrate the special moments of our lives, whether it's a birthday, some post-Iftaar treats in Ramadan, or simply something sweet and delicious to celebrate making it through a super-busy week!

SPICED PUMPKIN MUFFINS

These are such a great way to enjoy some fall flavors. I love cooking with pumpkin; it adds such great taste, ups the fiber content of your dish, and goes well with warming ingredients like cinnamon, dates, and honey.

MAKES 12 MUFFINS

1 cup pumpkin purée
⅓ cup maple syrup
2 eggs
1 teaspoon vanilla extract
¼ cup almond butter
1–2 medjool dates, pitted and soaked in water for 10–15 minutes
¼ cup unsweetened almond milk
2½ cups rolled oats
1 teaspoon baking powder
½ teaspoon baking soda
½ teaspoon salt
1 teaspoon ground cinnamon
½ cup dark chocolate chips

Preheat the oven to 350°F. Grease a 12-cup muffin pan with coconut oil or line it with paper liners.

In a blender, place all the ingredients—wet ingredients first, then dry—except for the chocolate chips. Blend on high until smooth (you may need to stop and stir a few times; the batter will be thick).

Pour the batter into a large bowl; it may heat as it blends, so pouring it into a bowl helps it to cool. When the batter is no longer warm, mix in the chocolate chips.

Pour the batter into the muffin cups. Bake for 12 to 15 minutes until a toothpick inserted in the center comes out clean. Turn the muffins out onto a rack and let cool for 10 minutes before serving (if you can wait that long).

The muffins will keep in an airtight container at room temperature for a few days and in the fridge for up to a week.

RAW CHOCOLATE BARS

This is my healthier version of a chocolate bar. Still definitely a treat, but made with more wholesome ingredients rather than all the junk found in regular candy. Once you have the basic recipe down, feel free to change it up. You can try switching out different nuts and nut butters (I use almond butter, but it also works well with peanut and cashew butter), tossing in some dried fruit, or adding interesting spices like cinnamon, dried ginger, or even cayenne!

MAKES 8 LARGE BARS

½ cup coconut oil
⅓ cup nut butter
½ cup cacao powder (see Tip)
½ cup maple syrup
1 teaspoon vanilla extract
Pinch of sea salt
¾ cup chopped raw walnuts, some reserved for topping
½ teaspoon flaky sea salt, for topping (optional)

Line an 8 × 8-inch baking pan with parchment.

In a large bowl, whisk the coconut oil and nut butter until smooth. Stir in the cacao powder until well combined. Mix in the maple syrup, vanilla, and sea salt and beat until all ingredients are well combined. Stir in the walnuts (reserving a few to sprinkle on top).

Pour the mixture into the prepared baking pan. Smooth out the mixture and sprinkle with the reserved walnuts and flaky sea salt, if using.

Cover and freeze for a few hours until set. Cut into eight bars. If you have any bars left over, you can place them in the fridge in an airtight container for up to 5 days.

TIP: This recipe calls for cacao powder, not cocoa powder. They are similar ingredients that both begin as beans from the cacao plant. But cacao powder is made from fermented cacao beans that have not been roasted, whereas cocoa powder is made from beans that have been roasted and processed at a higher temperature. As a result, cacao powder contains more nutrients than cocoa!

Almond Fudge Chocolate
Chip Cookies, p. 238

Spiced Pumpkin
Muffins, pg. 231

Flourless Chocolate
Banana Loaf, p. 235

Perfect Banana Oat
Cookies p. 236

FLOURLESS CHOCOLATE
BANANA LOAF OR MUFFINS

The batter for these amazing flourless muffins (or loaf) comes together in a snap; just toss everything but the chocolate chips into your blender, blend till smooth, and pour into your muffin or loaf pan. Before you know it, you'll be on your way to an irresistible chocolaty treat that is perfect for an afternoon pick-me-up (or even an indulgent breakfast).

MAKES 1 LOAF, 12 MUFFINS, OR 24 MINI MUFFINS

4 super-ripe bananas
2 eggs
1 cup rolled oats
½ cup almond butter
¼ cup honey
½ cup almond meal
1 medjool date, pitted
1 teaspoon baking soda
1 teaspoon ground cinnamon
2 teaspoons vanilla extract
¼ cup ground flaxseeds
½ cup semisweet chocolate chips (reserve a few for topping)
Coconut flakes, for topping

Preheat the oven to 375°F. Grease a loaf pan, 12-cup muffin pan, or a 24-cup mini muffin pan very well with coconut oil, or line it with paper liners.

In your blender, place all the ingredients in the order listed, except for the chocolate chips and coconut flakes. Blend on high until the batter is smooth.

Pour the batter into a large bowl; it may heat as it blends, so pouring it into a bowl helps it to cool. When the batter is no longer warm, mix in the chocolate chips.

Fill the loaf pan or each cup of the muffin pan three-quarters full with batter. Top with a chocolate chip and a sprinkle of coconut flakes. Bake for 40 minutes for a loaf or for 10 to 12 minutes for large muffins or 8 to 9 minutes for mini muffins, until a toothpick inserted in the center comes out clean.

Let the loaf or muffins cool for 10 to 15 minutes before enjoying. These can be stored in an airtight container at room temperature for a few days or in the fridge for up to a week . . . but good luck keeping them around that long.

PERFECT BANANA OAT COOKIES

You know when you're looking for an after-school treat that will keep the kids happy but won't have all the sugar? These cookies are just the thing. Assuming you're like me and have some bananas that are a little overripe sitting on your kitchen counter, you've probably got all the ingredients on hand to make this right now. Plus, you can whip them up in less than 20 minutes!

MAKES 12 COOKIES

2 very ripe bananas
2 cups rolled oats
½ cup peanut butter (or other nut butter of your choice)
1 tablespoon maple syrup
1 teaspoon vanilla extract
½ teaspoon salt
½ cup chocolate chips

Preheat the oven to 350°F. Line a rimmed baking sheet with parchment paper or a silicone liner.

In a mixing bowl, mash the bananas completely with a fork. Add the oats, peanut butter, maple syrup, vanilla, and salt and mix with your fork or a wooden spoon until well combined. Stir in the chocolate chips.

Drop mounds of dough by tablespoonfuls onto the cookie sheet, leaving 1 inch of space between the cookies.

Bake for 15 minutes or until the cookies are set at the edges and lightly browned. Let the cookies cool on the baking sheet for 5 minutes, then remove to a wire rack to cool completely.

Store the cookies in an airtight container for up to 5 days.

ALMOND FUDGE CHOCOLATE CHIP COOKIES

It took some time to get the recipe for these cookies just right. I wanted something that was chewy and chocolate but used less sugar, butter, and flour. Something I, or the kids, could whip up really fast and have some delicious chewy cookies in no time. Let me tell you, it was worth the trial and error—and now that the recipe has been perfected, the hardest part of making them is waiting for the oven to heat up! I can almost guarantee they will disappear in seconds, they're that good.

MAKES 12 TO 15 COOKIES

½ cup almond butter
⅔ cup brown sugar
¼ cup almond flour
1 large egg
1 teaspoon vanilla extract
1 teaspoon baking soda
½ teaspoon salt
½ cup sliced almonds
½ cup roughly chopped dark chocolate

In a large bowl, cream together the almond butter and brown sugar until well combined. Add the almond flour, egg, vanilla, baking soda, and salt and mix well. Fold in the sliced almonds and chocolate pieces.

Cover and chill the batter in the fridge for at least 1 hour up to overnight.

Preheat the oven to 350°F. Line a rimmed baking sheet with parchment paper or a silicone liner.

Scoop the dough by tablespoonfuls and place the balls 1 to 2 inches apart on the prepared baking sheet. Press down just a little to flatten the tops.

Bake for 9 minutes until the cookies are golden brown. Transfer to a wire rack to cool. Enjoy!

DATE BALLS

Packed with nuts and naturally sweet from the delicious dates and coconut, these date balls are a great energy snack that will keep you feeling full anytime; I make them every Ramadan because they're a perfect boost after you've been fasting all day. Make them on the weekend and enjoy them all week.

MAKES 18 TO 20 BALLS

1 cup medjool dates, pitted
1 cup almonds, whole
½ cup shredded coconut, unsweetened
1 tablespoon coconut oil
½ teaspoon sea salt
½ teaspoon ground cinnamon
½ teaspoon ground nutmeg

Soak the dates in a bowl of hot water until soft, for 10 to 15 minutes. Drain.

Pulse the nuts and coconut in a food processor until they've crumbled into a fine meal. Add the dates, coconut oil, sea salt, cinnamon, and nutmeg and pulse in the food processor again until the mixture becomes a crumbled texture.

Form the mixture into 1½-inch balls. Refrigerate to set their shape, for at least 10 to 15 minutes.

Keep in an airtight container in the fridge for up to a week.

Carrot Cake Balls, p. 241

Date Balls, p. 239

CARROT CAKE BALLS

These high-energy snacks have natural sweetness thanks to dates and coconut, with the flavors of a classic carrot cake. What's not to love? These are a great hearty snack to keep you going between meals or before a workout.

MAKES 18 TO 20 BALLS

1 cup medjool dates, pitted
1 cup rolled oats
½ cup grated carrots
½ cup whole almonds
⅓ cup shredded coconut
  flakes
¼ cup pecans
2 tablespoons cacao
  powder
1 teaspoon ground
  cinnamon
¼ cup nut butter (almond,
  hazelnut, or peanut)
1 tablespoon vanilla extract

Soak the dates in a bowl of hot water until soft, for 10 to 15 minutes. Drain.

Pulse the remaining ingredients in your food processor until well combined and finely chopped. Add the dates and pulse again to incorporate, scraping down the sides as needed.

Form into 1½-inch balls and refrigerate to set their shape, for 10 to 15 minutes.

Keep in an airtight container in the fridge for up to 5 days.

STUFFED DATES WITH
NUT BUTTER AND CHOCOLATE

These stuffed dates taste like a Snickers bar, but they're so much better for you! I love making these during Ramadan, when we have friends and family coming over to break their fasts. They are just so beautiful, the perfect sweet bite to serve at your next party as a dessert option.

MAKES 24 STUFFED DATES

14 ounces dark chocolate, melted (I like 70 percent dark chocolate)
24 medjool dates, pitted
¼ cup natural chunky peanut butter, hazelnut butter, or almond butter
Sea salt, for garnish
Crushed pistachios, for garnish

Break the chocolate into small pieces and place in a microwave-safe bowl. Melt the chocolate in the microwave in 30-second increments, stirring in between, so it doesn't burn. Or you could melt the chocolate in a double boiler or a large glass bowl set over a small pot of simmering water. Once the chocolate is completely melted, set the bowl aside.

Cut a slit in each date end to end. Pull each date apart slightly at the slit to make a little pocket. With a small spoon, scoop a bit of nut butter into each date.

Dip each date into the melted chocolate to lightly coat (you can do this with a fork or stick a toothpick into the date and dip it fondue-style). Place the chocolate-coated dates on a lined baking sheet. Sprinkle sea salt and pistachios on top of each date while the chocolate is still runny. Place the dates in the fridge for 30 minutes or until the chocolate is set.

Serve cold or allow the dates to come to room temperature. You can keep the dates in the fridge in an airtight container for up to 5 days.

GRANOLA YOGURT PARFAIT

Listen, I enjoy eating at cute little cafés and coffee shops as much as anyone else (I just love the way they make the food look as good as it tastes!), but I can't spend all my hard-earned dollars in fancy cafés, so it's well worth the few extra minutes to dress up this tasty treat at home to make it feel extra special. This homemade parfait is so simple to make: just assemble your favorite ingredients, layer them in a nice-looking glass or jar, and voilà! Sit by your favorite window and marvel at how you single-handedly brought the café vibes home while you enjoy this beauty along with your morning coffee.

MAKES 1 SERVING

¾ cup plain Greek yogurt
  or skyr
2 tablespoons granola
  (Chocolate Date Granola,
  page 29, or store-bought)
½ banana, sliced
⅓ cup berries
1½ teaspoons maple syrup
  (optional)
1 teaspoon chocolate
  shavings (optional)

In a mason jar or large glass, layer the yogurt, granola, and fruit (add a couple layers of each if you want it extra fancy). Drizzle the parfait with maple syrup and top with chocolate shavings if desired.

HEALTHY-ISH MANGO KULFI

Kulfi is the Indian version of ice cream. The combination of sweet and tangy, with a hint of saffron, and the smooth yet crunchy texture, with pieces of pistachio and almond, make this dessert so special. I decided to up the protein content and cut down on the added sugar, as mangoes are already pretty sweet to begin with. Serve it up like ice cream or as individual Popsicles. It's a hit every time!

MAKES 8 TO 10 KULFI

1 cup mango pulp (from a can), or 2 ripe mangoes, peeled, pitted, and cut into chunks
¾ cup Greek yogurt
½ cup condensed milk
1 tablespoon cardamom powder
¼ cup milk
Pinch of saffron
2 tablespoons chopped pistachios, for topping (optional)

In a blender, place the mango, yogurt, condensed milk, and cardamom powder and purée until smooth and everything is incorporated.

Pour the milk into a small microwave-safe bowl and add the saffron. Microwave on high for 45 seconds to release the color and flavor of the saffron (the milk will become a lovely yellow). Pour the milk into the mango mixture and mix. You will have a nice, thick mixture. Spoon this mixture into small plastic cups, Popsicle molds, or a large shallow plastic storage container. Freeze for at least 6 hours or overnight.

When you are ready to serve, remove from the freezer and let it sit for 5 minutes at room temperature. If you freeze the kulfi in a large container, cut it into squares. Top with the chopped pistachios if desired.

KHEER
(North Indian Rice Pudding)

It's amazing what happens when you just combine simple ingredients and cook them nice and slow; you can end up creating the richest dishes! This kheer is a perfect example—rice pudding for the soul. Kheer can be served warm or cold (I love mine chilled). The rose water is optional but adds a nice floral note to the pudding.

MAKES 6 SERVINGS

- ¼–⅓ **cup basmati rice (more rice will make the kheer thicker)**
- **1 teaspoon ghee**
- **3–4 green cardamom pods, slightly crushed**
- **1 quart whole milk**
- **4–5 tablespoons sugar**
- **3 tablespoons chopped cashews or almonds**
- **1½ teaspoons rose water (optional)**

Rinse the rice in a fine-mesh sieve until the water turns clear. Then place the rice in a large bowl, cover with cool water, and let it soak for 20 to 30 minutes. Drain the rice and set aside.

Heat the ghee in a large heavy-bottomed pan over medium heat. Add the rice and cardamom pods and cook, stirring constantly, until fragrant, for 2 minutes. Stir in the milk, increase the heat to medium-high, and bring the milk to a boil—this will take 10 to 12 minutes. Stir occasionally so that the rice doesn't stick to the bottom of the pan.

Simmer the kheer for about 25 minutes, stirring every couple of minutes, until most of the liquid is absorbed, the pudding is thick, and the rice is cooked through. If you want superthick kheer, cook for 15 more minutes at this point—but don't forget to stir! (The kheer will also continue to thicken as it cools.)

Mix in the sugar and nuts and cook for another 5 minutes until the sugar has dissolved completely.

Remove the pan from the heat. Stir in the rose water if desired. Garnish with more nuts and serve the kheer warm, or refrigerate for 4 to 5 hours and serve chilled.

SWEET POTATO BROWNIES

You will never believe that these gooey, chocolaty brownies have sweet potatoes in them! I'm all about enjoying sweet treats, and finding fun ways to increase the fiber and nutrition content in them just makes me and my family feel so much better. Don't worry, it'll be our little secret—nobody else needs to know!

MAKES 8 SQUARES

3–4 small sweet potatoes
2 large eggs
¾ cup brown sugar
3 ounces bittersweet chocolate, melted and cooled
¼ cup coconut oil
1 teaspoon vanilla extract
¼ cup cacao powder
½ teaspoon baking powder
½ teaspoon salt
½ cup chocolate chips

Preheat the oven to 350°F. Grease a 9 × 9-inch baking pan.

Poke the sweet potatoes a few times with a fork. Microwave on high until cooked through, for about 10 minutes depending on the size of your potatoes. Peel and mash the cooked sweet potatoes; discard the skins.

In a large bowl, beat the eggs and brown sugar with a hand mixer until they are fluffy and light.

Add the melted chocolate and coconut oil to the egg mixture and beat again to combine. Next, add the mashed sweet potatoes and vanilla; mix well to combine everything. Stir in the cacao powder, baking powder, and salt until well combined. Finally, fold in the chocolate chips.

Pour the batter into the prepared baking pan. Bake for 30 to 35 minutes until a toothpick inserted into the center comes out clean.

Allow the brownies to cool completely, then cut into squares and enjoy!

ONE-BOWL CHOCOLATE CAKE

This easy chocolate cake is a guaranteed crowd-pleaser, making it my go-to recipe for special dinners and get-togethers. Not to mention chocolate is my favorite sweet. It's a perfect base to decorate with frosting or to keep simple with just a dusting of confectioners' sugar and berries (or go all out with both!). Either way, I say: have your cake and eat it too!

MAKES 6 SERVINGS

Butter, for greasing the pan
¾ cup milk
1 tablespoon white vinegar
¾ cup vegetable oil
2 eggs
½ cup white sugar
1 cup brown sugar
1 cup all-purpose flour
¾ cup cocoa powder
1 tablespoon baking powder
1 teaspoon salt
½ cup boiling coffee

Preheat the oven to 325°F. Grease a 9-inch round baking pan with butter and set aside.

In a large bowl, first whisk the milk and vinegar until well combined. Then add the oil, eggs, and white and brown sugar and whisk. Add the flour, cocoa powder, baking powder, salt, and coffee. With a hand mixer or whisk, mix until the batter is nice and smooth.

Pour the batter into the prepared baking pan.

Bake for 50 minutes until a toothpick inserted in the center comes out clean. Allow the cake to cool on a rack for 20 minutes.

TIP: The same batter can be used to bake 12 cupcakes. Pour the batter into a 12-cup muffin pan that has been well greased or lined with paper liners and bake for 12 to 15 minutes.

SAFFRON OLIVE OIL CAKE

This moist, light olive oil cake is the perfect pairing with a cup of coffee or tea. The saffron and orange zest add a unique bright and flowery flavor and the prettiest tint of gold. If you're looking for something a bit different that's going to wow your friends and family, this cake is the jewel you'll be bringing to the table.

MAKES 8 SERVINGS

1 cup all-purpose flour
½ cup almond flour
½ teaspoon baking powder
½ teaspoon baking soda
½ teaspoon of salt
3 eggs
1¼ cups sugar
¼ cup orange or lemon juice
¾ cup olive oil
½ cup milk
¼ teaspoon saffron strands, ground
1–2 teaspoons orange or lemon zest
½ teaspoon vanilla extract
Confectioners' sugar, for dusting

Preheat the oven to 350°F. Grease the bottom and sides of a 9-inch round cake pan and line the bottom with a circle of parchment paper.

In a large bowl, mix the flours, baking powder, baking soda, and salt.

In a separate bowl, whisk the eggs, sugar, and orange juice well until light and frothy. Continue to whisk as you add the oil, milk, saffron, zest, and vanilla.

Pour the flour mixture into the wet ingredients and stir until everything is incorporated. Pour the batter into your prepared cake pan and bake for 45 to 50 minutes until a toothpick inserted into the center comes out clean.

Invert the cake onto a rack and remove the parchment paper. Let the cake cool completely.

Dust with icing sugar.

TIP: You can top this elegant cake so many different ways. Try it with candied citrus and decorative edible flowers. Or try fresh berries tossed in a bit of orange juice and ground pistachios.

HEALTHY RAMADAN GUIDE
APPRECIATING OUR BODIES AS A BLESSING

RAMADAN IS A MONTH WHERE MUSLIMS FAST from sunrise to sunset. It is a month of spiritual growth, prayer, and reflection as well as a time to reconnect with family, friends, and community. There are so many spiritual benefits to fasting and so much wisdom and beauty behind this holy month. But while we all anticipate and eagerly embrace the spiritual aspects of Ramadan, many of us struggle year after year with some of the physical challenges that this month brings. Some people worry about how they're going to make it through the long days while working or taking care of their families, while others are afraid that they will lose the health gains they've made over the past year. No matter where you are, it's true that Ramadan certainly presents its own unique set of challenges.

Our bodies are incredible biological machines, and like any finely tuned machine, they need clean fuel to perform at peak levels. Once we realize that our food is actually just fuel for our bodies, we become more mindful about what it is that we're consuming. Taking care of our bodies isn't just an act of self-love and personal empowerment—it is also an act of devotion. There's a hadith in which the Prophet (S.A.W.) said: "Your body has a right over you." Alhamdulillah we have been blessed with these incredible bodies and it is our responsibility to take care of them. What better time to express gratitude for our bodies than in this holy month?

This section aims to help you figure out just exactly how to eat healthy during Ramadan. Obviously, there is no one-size-fits-all approach to this, but there are definitely some general principles to keep in mind when considering your meals and snacks during Ramadan.

BREAK THE RULES EVERY NOW AND THEN

It's great to set lofty goals for yourself during this blessed month, but don't be too hard on yourself if you don't win each and every night. Put it this way: no matter how pure your intentions, you'll still probably lose your temper every now and then, or find your mind wandering during the odd prayer, and you might not finish the entire Quran like you had planned to. That's okay. Remember, at the end of the day we're only human. In the same way, don't stress out when you break some of these food rules every now and then. Try to eat mostly healthy foods but also plan on having some treats (what I call the 80:20 rule).

There's no point stressing out just because things aren't perfect (they never will be!); just do your best and keep on Ramadan'ing.

SUHOOR

One of the most common questions I'm asked is "What can I eat at Suhoor time that will keep me feeling full throughout the day?" Sorry to say, but the simple answer, my dears, is: Nothing! Unfortunately, there's no possible meal that you can eat that will keep you from feeling hungry over the course of a sixteen- to seventeen-hour fast (the human body just doesn't work like that). But there are definitely a few rules you can follow if you want to prepare the most sustaining meals that will help keep your body feeling full and energized longer.

As you may have guessed, I do not recommend skipping Suhoor. But breakfast doesn't have to be complicated (in fact, some of my go-to Suhoor recipes are as simple as you can get). The key is to try to get in as many good healthy nutrients and calories in that one meal as you can. I definitely aim to get a good mix of proteins, complex carbohydrates, and healthy fats. I also make sure to drink two full glasses of water at Suhoor time.

Here are some of my favorite Suhoor recipes:

IFTAAR

When breaking fast, most people tend to think the best strategy is "eat as much as you can, as fast as you can." A much better Iftaar strategy, however, is to pace yourself. Trust me, this simple change alone will make such a huge difference in the way you feel for the rest of the night. I usually start with a date (khajoor) and a full glass of water to break my fast (I also sip more water during the rest of my Iftaar). Rather than jumping straight to the main course, I love starting first with something lighter, such as soups or salads. We also try to have some fruits at each Iftaar. Here are some lighter recipes:

Spiced Chickpea and Cauliflower Salad with Lemony Tahini Dressing (page 113)

Bright Summer Kale Salad (page 114)

Lentil and Parsley Salad (page 120)

Fresh Greek Pasta Salad (page 125)

Grilled Corn and Zucchini Salad (page 126)

Mango, Feta, and Greens (page 129)

I know the fasts are long and by Iftaar time you're . . . well, hungry! Not to mention, you may have been invited to Iftaars where you feel the temptation (and obligation) to try a little of everything. Remember that your stomach has likely shrunk from fasting all day, so by taking it slowly, you will give your body more time to process the signals coming from your digestive tract that let you know when you're full (so you won't overeat). Instead of overstuffing yourself at Iftaar time, aim to have a generous-sized meal but leave space for smaller meals/snacks through the rest of the night. Try some of these:

Tuna Kebabs (page 66)

My Go-to Dal Curry (page 135)

Aloo Gobi (Indian Potato and Cauliflower Curry) (page 136)

Palak Tofu (Spinach Tofu Curry) (page 139)

Lazy Lasagna (page 140)

Masala Fish with Indian Potatoes (page 149)

Masala Shrimp Wraps (page 150)

Thai-Style Shrimp Coconut Curry (page 155)

Kuku Paka (Coconut Chicken Curry with Potatoes) (page 163)

Sheet Pan Sumac Chicken with Carrots and Cauliflower (page 164)

Chicken and Yellow Rice (page 167)

Seekh Kebabs (page 175)

EID

Eid Mubarak! The Hunger Games are officially over, and just like Katniss you've emerged stronger and wiser than ever. Now it's Eid and I give you full permission to go out and enjoy! Enjoy the multiple servings of baklava and mithai, throw down a midday meal of biryani, and get that fancy specialty coffee you've been craving. Remember, enjoyment and indulging are an essential part of a healthy and fulfilling life. It's all about balance, right?! Here are some of my favorite treats to celebrate with:

Healthy-ish Mango Kulfi (page 246)

Kheer (North Indian Rice Pudding) (page 249)

One-Bowl Chocolate Cake (page 253)

Saffron Olive Oil Cake (page 254)

Ramadan is the most blessed time of the year. I pray that we are able to carry forward the lessons (both spiritual and physical) of Ramadan into our everyday lives Insha'Allah. Hopefully this Ramadan you made the decision to be more mindful of what you were eating, made healthier food choices, drank more water, worked out more regularly, and felt a deeper connection with and gratitude for your body.

METRIC CONVERSIONS

THE RECIPES IN THIS BOOK HAVE NOT BEEN tested with metric measurements, so some variations might occur.

Remember that the weight of dry ingredients varies according to the volume or density factor: 1 cup of flour weighs far less than 1 cup of sugar, and 1 tablespoon doesn't necessarily hold 3 teaspoons.

General Formula for Metric Conversion

Ounces to grams	multiply ounces by 28.35
Grams to ounces	multiply ounces by 0.035
Pounds to grams	multiply pounds by 453.5
Pounds to kilograms	multiply pounds by 0.45
Cups to liters	multiply cups by 0.24
Fahrenheit to Celsius	subtract 32 from Fahrenheit temperature, multiply by 5, divide by 9
Celsius to Fahrenheit	multiply Celsius temperature by 9, divide by 5, add 32

Volume (Liquid) Measurements

1 teaspoon = ⅙ fluid ounce = 5 milliliters

1 tablespoon = ½ fluid ounce = 15 milliliters

2 tablespoons = 1 fluid ounce = 30 milliliters

¼ cup = 2 fluid ounces = 60 milliliters

⅓ cup = 2 ⅔ fluid ounces = 79 milliliters

½ cup = 4 fluid ounces = 118 milliliters

1 cup or ½ pint = 8 fluid ounces = 250 milliliters

2 cups or 1 pint = 16 fluid ounces = 500 milliliters

4 cups or 1 quart = 32 fluid ounces = 1,000 milliliters

1 gallon = 4 liters

Volume (Dry) Measurements

¼ teaspoon = 1 milliliter

½ teaspoon = 2 milliliters

¾ teaspoon = 4 milliliters

1 teaspoon = 5 milliliters

1 tablespoon = 15 milliliters

¼ cup = 59 milliliters

⅓ cup = 79 milliliters

½ cup = 118 milliliters

⅔ cup = 158 milliliters

¾ cup = 177 milliliters

1 cup = 225 milliliters

4 cups or 1 quart = 1 liter

½ gallon = 2 liters

1 gallon = 4 liters

ACKNOWLEDGMENTS

FIRST AND FOREMOST, I WANT TO EXPRESS MY deepest and most heartfelt gratitude to my community. It's *your* support that's allowed me to share my passion for food and fitness. Your encouragement and all the positive vibes you've shared with me were the inspiration behind this book. I've always cherished sharing my love for food with loved ones, and I consider all of you to be an extension of my own family. I wish I could cook up these dishes, sit across a table, and share them with each of you.

A special thank-you to my husband, Zishan (also known as Zee). Your love and support mean the world to me. You've worn so many different hats, from recipe tester to late-night editor, and everything in between. You've been my biggest supporter from day one, and no dream of mine has ever been too big for you. I love you :).

To my wonderful children, Ahmed and Asiyah, thank you for being my biggest cheerleaders. I cherish the way your eyes light up when you walk into the kitchen and smell your favorite dish. I love that you enjoy cooking with me, learning the recipes I watched my mom make (as well as some other new creations).

To Yasaman Haj-Shafiei. You know you're incredibly lucky when your work bestie feels like your little sister. I couldn't have imagined a better, kinder person to share my career dreams with.

A heartfelt thank-you to my book agent, Kim Lindman. Thank you for believing in this idea from the very beginning and for always being there to support me. Your calm presence was exactly what I needed when things felt chaotic.

To my editor and publisher at Hachette Go, Renée Sedliar: I feel truly blessed that we had the opportunity to work together on this project. Your enthusiasm, constant encouragement, and joy every time we discussed the book helped me immensely through the process of writing it.

Thanks to the amazing team at Hachette: Cisca Schreefel, Shubhani Sarkar, Nyamekye Waliyaya, Nzinga Temu, Michael Barrs, Amanda Kain, Mary Ann Naples, Michelle Aielli, and Claire Schulz.

Ceri Marsh, from the initial concept to the final edits, you've made the book-writing process not only efficient but also incredibly enjoyable. Beyond being a great friend, your ability to help me get my thoughts and ideas into words has been invaluable.

Joanna Wojewoda, thank you for taking the most stunning pictures. I've never seen my food and my family look so beautiful. You've perfectly captured the heart and soul of my recipes, and for that I'm deeply grateful.

To my incredible team in the kitchen: thanks so much to Stu, Sarah, Anar, Naila, Muneera, and Sukaina for all your invaluable help and support.

And finally, to my parents.

Immigrating to Canada from Kenya must not have been easy, but you did it to give your children a better life. Those sacrifices made it possible for me to chase my dreams. You grounded me in our culture and faith, and I'm determined to carry that legacy forward with my children. Thank you for all you've done.

Special thanks to my recipe testers: Lahari Jay, Fatema Rai, Zainab Alsamarae, Stephanie Stuerle, Mahmuda Khan, Muneera Haji, Melissa Marchioni, Kaniz Khaki, Aasia Fazal, Anna Morellato, Selina Merali, Rashmi Sarkaria, Farzana Khimji , rabiya fahmi, Lydia Jean, Shaista Ali, Fatim Ajwani, Amani Abdallah , Gurpreet Ram, Noor Siddiqi, Aliya Dharamshi, Sharmin Ahmed, Amy Harik, Zeinab Moazin, and Eiman Habib.

INDEX

ABOUT THE AUTHOR

AS A TRAINER AND WELLNESS INFLUENCER, ZEHRA ALLIBHAI has been inspiring women to be healthy, active, and confident for over fifteen years. She lives in Toronto with her husband and their two children.